Randy Benjamin

FREE Internet

Randy Benjamin

Other books available on Amazon by Randy Benjamin

"How To Transfer Cassettes To CD"
"How To Publish Anything On The Amazon Kindle"
"Tapestries" (Children's Album and Book)
"The Healthy Computer"
"The Internet Guide Handbook"
"More Of The Internet Guide"
"The Healthy Computer"
"Original Songs" An Album of original songs
"Anomaly" (Summer of 2010)

FREE Internet

Randy Benjamin

FREE Internet
An Intguide Publication

All rights reserved, including the right to reproduce this book or portions thereof in any form whatsoever. For additional information, address Randy Benjamin:

Subsidiary Rights
Randy Benjamin
60 Thompson Drive
Vincennes, IN 47591

Copyright © 2009 by Randy Benjamin

13 digit ISBN: 978-0-9679361-3-0
www.randybenjamin.com

Printed in the United States of America

FREE Internet

Contents

Page   Heading

09   In The Beginning
12   The Basics – Where and How
16   Free Internet and Open Connections
21   How Hard Is It To Steal Someone's Internet
23   When Is The Internet FREE
27   A Simple WI-FI Reflector
35   Two YAGI Antennas For Medium Range
49   YAGI Loop Antenna
59   Modifying The Belkin USB Adapter
64   The Parabolic Satellite Dish
72   WI-FI CANnon
80   The Dish/WI-FI CANnon Combo
84   Keep Your Own AP From Being Compromised
88   Author Bio
90   Excerpt from "Anomaly"
93   How To Publish Anything On Amazon's Kindle
94   How To Transfer Cassettes To CD
95   Original Songs CD

Preface

This book is divided into four parts. The first part gives you a little history about the Internet, especially the wireless side of it. I'll keep it short, I promise.

The second part, will explain how you can find thousands of FREE wireless access points (AP) scattered around the country. I also discuss the difference between FREE access points, and "open" access points. There is a difference. Though many times, they can be one and the same. In the third part of the book, I'll show you how to build inexpensive, (sometimes free) high-gain antennas out of things you have around the house, (cardboard, aluminum foil, coat hangers, tin cans, etc.) that will allow you to pick-up FREE Internet access from blocks to even miles away.

In the last part, I'll show you how to protect your home connection by turning on your router's encryption setting. Unless you configure your router's encryption, anyone within 300 feet, (and a mile or more with one of these DIY antennas) can log onto your Internet connection just like they were sitting in a chair next to you!

Before we get started...I want to warn you that stealing Internet from someone is against the law. At least in most places. But because it's such a new problem, few authorities enforce the laws pertaining to it. And since most people don't realize when it's happening, it mostly goes unreported. This makes it a very hard, almost impossible law to enforce.

Add to this that a lot of people could care less if their Internet connection is being compromised and purposely leave it 'open' so that others can log onto it. If all of this is beginning to sound confusing, that's because it is. This is another reason why 'Internet theft' is pretty low on the list of problems that law enforcement has to deal with. You mostly only hear of it if the case involves the theft of credit card or social security numbers. Rarely is anyone arrested for logging onto a wide open Internet connection.

Still, it is illegal in most places. I've included a few instances where someone actually has been arrested for using an unauthorized Internet connection, but they are far and few between.

That said, hacking into a 'secured' Internet connection (One using WEP, WAP, or some other form of encryption.) is a horse of a different color. This definitely is ILLEGAL! The antennas in this book could easily be used in illegal hacking. It's about like anything else. You can read a book, or knock someone over the head with it. It just depends on how you use the information I'm providing that determines the legalities.

So, with this in mind…let's get started with a little history of what we're dealing with and then get down to the real business of how to snag those FREE Internet connections.

ACKNOWLEDGEMENT

I'd like to thank, Nanette Grumieaux, for her help in editing the FREE Internet manuscript. Her input helped me to clarify many of the passages that would otherwise have been very confusing.

In The Beginning

The Internet was designed by a few visionaries back in the 60s. Scientists at MIT realized that it would be advantageous to the scientific community if the computers they were working with had a way to share information easily.

About the same time, the military (DARPA) saw that it would be of great interest to them as well and they bankrolled much of the development.

The earliest Internet was called ARPANET and it ran over the telephone lines. It wasn't easy to use, but it worked. Of course, everything back then was hard-wired. Over the years, new software protocols were invented with much of the research supported by military grants.

In those early years (60s and 70s) the basics that we use today (FTP, TCP/IP, Ethernet, Telnet, and UNIX) were invented, and routers were designed to distribute packets of information over this new medium even if part of the network was down.

Two forms of computer communications used during those early years rivaled the Internet we use today…USENET, a system allowing UNIX based computers to share information and BITNET, used by IBM mainframes to share information and provide the first email services.

In 1986, the National Science Foundation started NSFNET. This is the backbone that today's Internet is built on. Of course, it was still telephone based in 1986, but things would progress at breakneck speed from then on.

The first personal computers hit the market in the early 70s, and by the late 80s, they were really catching on with the general public. The problems with hardware standardization were solved when IBM entered the personal computer arena. Between IBM and Microsoft…computers were getting to the place where the average person could operate them without having to have a college degree in computer science.

By the mid 90s, anyone with a telephone connection and a modem could get on the Internet. Microsoft and a host of smaller companies were producing software (browsers, email clients, word processors, spread sheets, etc.) that fueled the home computer market. Around that same time, hardware manufacturers were racing to keep up with the exploding demand for ever faster computers. As the need to share data between users grew, so did the on-line industry. My first modem could operate at a speed of about 300 BPS. Within a few years, this had improved to 56,000 BPS. But that was as good as it would get.

The problem was with the phone lines. They were never designed to carry digital transmissions and there was a limit on how fast they could manage it. It was agonizing having to wait for those slow downloads. If someone sent you a picture, it might take an hour or more to download it. At this point you were stuck. You couldn't do anything until the download had completed.

My Internet connection today is 10 million BPS. Imagine that compared to 56,000. That's 178 times faster than the old dialup connection. To put this in perspective, if it takes one minute to download a picture now, it would have taken almost three hours to download that same picture on dialup.

Of course, dialup connections are still around. And they still have that same 56K limit. I do a lot of work on computers located out in the 'boonies' where cable or DSL won't reach, so I still see a lot of dialup connections. Satellite access has moved into some of this market but it's expensive. There's a big difference in the cost between dialup and broadband connections. I've seen dialup connections for as low as $7 a month. Some DSL (telephone based, but delivered by heavier gauge copper wire or fiber optic cable) subscriptions start around $18 per month. The problem with DSL is that it only works within about a three mile distance of the central office so unless you're close enough, you won't be able to get it. This range can be extended using a repeater, but there has to be enough clients to make installing one profitable for the DSL provider. Out in the country, that's usually not the case.

Cable Internet is generally priced in the $30 to $60 a month range and satellite is usually a little higher. Plus, you may have to buy or lease the equipment necessary to use a satellite connection. Even though it's S-L-O-W, the bottom line is…dialup is still better than nothing.

Wireless Internet

Wireless routers for personal computers have been around since the mid 90s, but they really didn't become popular until the WI-FI Alliance setup a list of procedures for interoperability called the IEE802.11 standards. When this happened, all of the manufacturers began building products that could 'talk' to each other. Because of that, wireless routers really began to catch on. The first time WI-FI was used commercially was in 1999. So even though wireless had been around for a few years, it really wasn't all that popular until the millennium.

OK, enough history. I'm sure you pretty much know the rest of the story. Let's get down to finding those FREE Internet sources.

The Basics – Where and How

Before you can log onto a FREE Internet provider, you've got to be able to find one. Let's start by using the Net to see what's out there. What we're looking for are WI-FI- "hotspots." Hotspot is a nickname for free wireless APs. (Access Points) There are several 'hotspot locaters' on-line that track WI-FI hotspots around the world. I'm going to list a few here that I've personally used and have worked well for me.

The one problem all of these 'locaters' have in common is in keeping their databases updated. So many new hotspots come online daily that it's nearly impossible to have a truly current listing. If you check back with these 'locaters' every few days, you'll probably find additional hotspots listed. It's a never ending battle trying to stay on top of things. Here are a few locaters you should check out:

1. **WI-FI FREESPOT:** http://www.wififreespot.com/
This locater's directory of FREE Wi-Fi hotspots in the US is broken down by State. They also list hotspots around the world. The directory listings are divided into five categories.
   a. Companies with multiple locations
   b. Airports
   c. Hotels, Motels, Inns and Resorts with National and Regional Chains.
   d. RV Parks and Campgrounds
   e. Vacation Rental Properties

When traveling, I use this site extensively. On my last trip to California, I knew in advance which motels I'd be staying at because I knew which ones had free Internet service. I just checked the website for the hotspots in the towns I'd be visiting.

2. **OPENWiFiSPOTS:** http://www.openwifispots.com/
You'll find another comprehensive directory of FREE wireless hotspots here. It's also one of the most up-to-date because the public does most of the updating and verifying. They claim to have over 25,000 hotspot listings in the US.

If you type in your city, state, and zip, you'll get a listing of any FREE APs in your area. I just did this for Vincennes and found two new hotspots I didn't know about. There's also a link to nearby towns. This is a great resource for finding local FREE APs.

(Tip) Be sure to check with several different locaters when you do a "hotspot" search. I just tried a new link called **Wi-FiHotSpotlist.com** http://www.wi-fihotspotlist.com/ and it didn't show a single hotspot in Vincennes! Obviously, not all of these locaters are using the same resources.

3. **JIWIRE:** http://v4.jiwire.com/search-hotspot-locations.htm

This is probably the ultimate when it comes to finding Wi-Fi hotspots. They list over 262,000 free and pay Wi-Fi location worldwide. And it really is a neat website. When you log onto the site, you'll be presented with a map of the continents of the world. I clicked on North America. Then I clicked on the United States. A US map appeared with blue circles scattered across it. The circles had numbers in them. Some numbers were as small as 2, others were as high as 5,000. I moved the cursor over southern Indiana and double clicked the mouse. This zoomed in on the map. After doing this a few more times, I had Vincennes, IN centered on the page. There were five smaller circles on top of Vincennes. Four of them were green, and one was blue. The green circles represented FREE Internet; the blue one was a pay site. When you move the curser over a circle, a message is displayed telling you the name of the AP and its street address. This really is a nice program.

4. Hotspot Sniffers: Checking with Internet locaters is one way to discover FREE hotspots near you; another is to use a device known as a Hotspot Sniffer, sometimes called a Hotspot Finder. I've been using one of these for the last five years and it has never let me down. These devices are small. The one I have is made by Zyxel. It's a tad bigger than a USB Flash Drive, about 4" long and 1" wide. This one doubles as an access point as well as a Wi-Fi finder. I can plug it into a USB port on my desktop computer and it will broadcast a Wi-Fi signal to my laptop.

Sniffers come in a couple of varieties. Some are really simple and just register the presence of an AP when it receives a signal. These usually have four or five LEDs that light up as the signal gets stronger. But the better ones will give you detailed information about any APs its found. My sniffer for instance tells me the SSID, transmitting channel, signal strength, encryption status and type, and whether the network is open or closed, all in a little LCD window. In the days before sniffers, you'd have needed a laptop to get this kind of information. And that could be dangerous if you were looking for an open connection while driving.

For all of the things these devices do, they are fairly inexpensive. I bought mine on eBay, used! I'm looking on eBay right now and there are several new and used ones listed. One similar to mine (A 'used' Trendnet Wi-Fi sniffer.) with the same features, just sold for $22.99 including shipping. New, they are going for $45 to $50 shipping included. The 'sniffers' that only show when an AP is near and its signal strength can be purchased on eBay for under $10, shipping included.

FREE Internet

I wouldn't dream of traveling without my Wi-Fi sniffer. I can pull up next to a restaurant, motel, library, etc., and immediately know if they have a FREE Internet connection. Of course, what it's really telling me is that it's either encrypted or 'open.' Open meaning one that I can log onto without a password. In reality, it might be that someone just never configured the encryption on their router. In that case, it might, or it might not be free. If I just needed to check my email, I'd most likely use it. Hopefully, it's a restaurant; and I can stop and have a cup of coffee while I'm at it. But there's no way to know if it's really FREE or just OPEN unless I see a sign saying so, or actually take the time to ask someone.

This is probably as good a time as any to get into what really constitutes a FREE Internet connection.

Free Internet and Open Connections

I hope you read the DISCLAIMER earlier stating, "The information in this book can easily be used to log onto your neighbor's unsecured Internet connection (which is illegal in most places) so please, DON'T abuse what you learn here."

You don't have to be a lawyer to know that it's not ethical to 'steal' your neighbor's Internet signal. But sometimes, it's hard not too. I've known cases where people were using their neighbor's Internet for years before they realized it. It's not all that hard to do. In fact, it's quite common.

I've been a computer technician for over 35 years and I've seen some pretty weird things happen. Case in point…I once found that a client's son had been using the neighbor's Internet ever since they gave him a laptop almost two years earlier. Here's how it happened. The parents had been using the same broadband carrier for several years. When their son started high school, they bought him a new laptop and added a wireless router to their desktop computer so he could log onto it.

The boy had a desk in his bedroom and that's mostly where he used the computer. When he first turned it on, a window appeared saying, "Searching for wireless connections." Then it said, "Wireless connections found, click here to view available networks." He clicked on the icon and saw two networks listed. He clicked on the top one. It said, "Connected to Linksys network" and the window went away. He clicked on IE, setup his Yahoo email account, and never thought much about it again. Every time he'd turn on his computer it would automatically connect to the Linksys network and he'd be good-to-go.

Almost two years later, he got a virus that was playing havoc with his computer. His parents called me to clear it up. I noticed on arriving that they had a D-Link router sitting on top of their computer. Upon inspecting the boy's laptop, I found that he had Norton anti-virus (came with the computer) installed but he had never registered it. The anti-virus software that ships with most computers is a limited 'trial' version and only updates the anti-virus database for 30 to 90 days. After that, you have to register it and pay for the updates. Because he'd never done this, his virus definitions were almost two years out-of-date. No wonder he was having problems. I deleted the Norton's (Great anti-virus program but NOT free.) software and installed AVG. AVG has a FREE version that is excellent and the virus definitions are free as well. You can find it at: http://free.avg.com/us-en/get-basic-protection. After removing the Norton software and installing AVG, I needed to reboot his laptop.

On rebooting, I noticed that it said, "Connecting to Linksys network." I thought, *hmmm*, something's not right here. I looked at the "wireless networks available" and sure enough, there were two of them. One was Linksys and the other was D-link. Neither was encrypted. Both were wide open to the world. It turned out that the neighbor's computer was sitting in a room facing the boy's bedroom, hardly twenty feet away. The neighbor's signal coming in through the window was actually stronger than the router signal in the living room which had to go through several walls before reaching his laptop. For the last two years, neither the neighbor, nor the boy had any idea that he was connected to the wrong Internet.

I encrypted their router and logged the boy's computer onto it. This was an honest case of not realizing that he was actually borrowing the neighbor's Internet connection. I've seen this happen many times over the years but it's the exception. Most of the time, people don't use someone else's Internet by mistake, they actively look for these 'open' Wi-Fi connections. It's illegal and unethical, but it's so easy to do and the perpetrator is so unlikely to get caught, that it's a very common occurrence in real life. If the truth be known, it's probably rampant everywhere.

It's somewhat similar to the problem of downloading music over the Net. In 2008, there was something like 2,500 people prosecuted for downloading music which is protected by copyright laws. But it was estimated that during this same time period, over 33 billion songs were illegally downloaded. (Based on the RIAA estimate) You have a better chance of getting struck by lightning or winning the Power Ball than you did getting caught downloading music.

Usually, when a case does make the news, it's because of stupidity. These people were so obvious that you couldn't miss them. Here are a few examples I ran across on a Google search.

There was a case in Florida in 2005 where a homeowner happened to look out his window and saw a man sitting in an SUV busily typing away on his laptop computer. After a few hours of this, he figured the man was stealing his Internet and called the police. The man was arrested and charged with *unauthorized access to a computer network*, a third-degree felony.

Another case involved a man accused of stealing Wi-Fi in Michigan. The laws in each state vary. This man was prosecuted under these Michigan statutes.

FRAUDULENT ACCESS TO COMPUTERS, COMPUTER SYSTEMS, AND COMPUTER NETWORKS (EXCERPT)
Act 53 of 1979

752.795 Prohibited conduct.

Sec. 5.

A person shall not intentionally and without authorization or by exceeding valid authorization do any of the following:

(a) Access or cause access to be made to a computer program, computer, computer system, or computer network to acquire, alter, damage, delete, or destroy property or otherwise use the service of a computer program, computer, computer system, or computer network.

(b) Insert or attach or knowingly create the opportunity for an unknowing and unwanted insertion or attachment of a set of instructions or a computer program into a computer program, computer, computer system, or computer network, that is intended to acquire, alter, damage, delete, disrupt, or destroy property or otherwise use the services of a computer program, computer, computer system, or computer network. This subdivision does not prohibit conduct protected under section 5 of article I of the state constitution of 1963 or under the first amendment of the constitution of the United States.

This guy ended up getting a fine of $400 plus he had to perform 40 hours of community service. But if he hadn't been such a nutcase, he probably would never have been caught. The place he was stealing the Internet from had observed him doing it from his car for several days. They actually asked him to leave on two different occasions, and he did, but then he'd come back a short time later. Finally, they called the police.

The police showed up and questioned the guy for about an hour but didn't arrest him. They did tell him to leave though. Which he did, but a few hours later; there he was again and in the exact same spot. Of course, this was too much. When the police came the second time, they hauled him off to jail! What a dummy!

I also found that a man was arrested in Chiswick, London in August of 2007 and charged with stealing a home owner's unsecured wireless Internet connection. This was part of a law passed in 2003 called, 'The Computer Misuse Act.'

Every country has its own laws and they are often quite different. It's getting someone to enforce them that's the problem. There are so many people logging onto these open connections, and so few officials to investigate…that when someone actually does get caught and prosecuted, it often makes the nightly news.

FREE Internet

How Hard Is It To Steal Someone's Internet

Well, that depends on how computer savvy the people involved are. If the person who owns a wireless router doesn't encrypt it, then there's a good chance that they are going to be taken advantage of. That's especially true if they live in a populated area. Apartment houses are notorious for Internet theft…as are trailer parks. Anywhere that residences are close together, you're likely going to find "open" Wi-Fi access points and most likely, someone other than the owner using them.

Over the years it's not been unusual for me to observe several neighbors getting together to 'share' a Wi-Fi connection. Even without special 'high-gain' antennas, a Wi-Fi signal will travel up to 300 feet. If placed in the right spot, this signal might be available to several neighbors living nearby. In an apartment complex, a dozen or more people might be able to take advantage of one router.

With service charges running from $30 to $60 a month, sharing this cost between several people can look pretty inviting. Ten people might put up $5 a month and they'd all have a high-speed connection. Even 'home' routers can theoretically serve 255 clients. Of course, the more people actively using a connection, the slower it will be. It's not likely that everyone would be downloading something at the same time. They might be writing a letter or listening to music. Just because they are all sharing the same Internet connection doesn't mean that they are all on it at the same time. With many Wi-Fi providers boasting download speeds of from 5 to 15 megabytes, there's a lot of bandwidth to go around.

The real loser here is the ISP, the Internet Service Provider. Think of it like you would cable TV. In fact, many cable TV suppliers now provide telephone and Internet service as well.

I've know several people who spliced into cable lines to share cable television. This is usually not easily done and the cable company has ways to detect it. Cable companies are always running ads warning people that stealing cable TV is illegal.

Stealing (or sharing) a wireless signal is much easier than splicing into a cable. In most cases, you just turn on your wireless device, and there it is. No wires to run or cables to splice. Nothing to hide from anyone, it's just there, coming in over the airwaves just like your radio. One way the ISP can detect that something is amiss is if an unusually large amount of Internet 'traffic' is reported by one client. Again, the key word here is, "IF." Of course, the ISP would have to be monitoring its subscribers in order to find this out and I don't know of any who are doing this…at least, not in my neck of the woods.

Here's an interesting story about a client that hired me to setup his computer system in Florida several years ago. He had just purchased a mobile home park with 200 units in it. Of these, about 75 were permanent locations for trailers and the other 125 were for RVs and campers. Some had full electric and others were primitive. This was a two million dollar investment. He hired me to setup his computer so he could manage the rental units using QuickBooks.

As I was leaving, he told me of an idea that was going to make him a ton of extra money. His office was in the center of the park. He was going to install a router above his office on a pole about 25 feet in the air. He would offer Internet (encrypted of course) to his renters on a basis of $2 a night, $10 a week, or $25 a month. He figured he would be able to average a minimum of $3,000 a month pure profit with this setup. Not bad for an investment of $70 for the wireless router, maybe $30 for the pole, and another $50 for the wire and enclosure to make it waterproof. He was paying $55 a month at the time for unlimited

Internet service. I don't know if it worked or not, but I don't see any reason why it wouldn't have. Again, it was the ISP who was losing money in this scenario.

These are all examples of people abusing the system. Some are more creative than others, and some border on being illegal while others are definitely illegal. It's how strictly the laws are enforced that seems to be the deciding factor in most occurrences.

When Is The Internet FREE

Even this can be hard to judge. If the town officials have decided that it's in the towns best interest to provide FREE Internet for the residents, and you're a citizen of the town…then you should be fine in using the facilities provided. But wait…what if (like in my home town) the FREE Internet access is only setup for the downtown business district? Does this mean I can only use it if I happen to be downtown? What if I live a block or two away and can pick up the signal? Is it still OK? What if I live two or three miles away…or more?

Is it really just for the downtown residents? That doesn't seem fair. Maybe the city planners just decided to start with the downtown district and are planning on branching out as funds become available? Who knows? But as far as I'm concerned, if it is free to the downtown residents, and I can receive it too, I'll use it.

[(Note) *I just started editing this manuscript at one of our local parks. I usually go to the University coffee shop to write when I want to get away from my desk. But it's a beautiful day out and I thought the park would be nice. I'm mentioning this now because a box just popped up saying, "new connection found."*

I clicked on the "view available wireless connections" option and found that the city has installed FREE WI-FI here at the park. So, here's another FREE connection for the local residents. This was a pleasant surprise.]

These are questions that haven't really been answered officially yet. This is all so new that there are very few precedents on which to draw from. Here's another thing to consider.

Many businesses are setting up FREE Internet for their customers. Does this mean that I have to come inside to be eligible to use the FREE service? What if I just sit in my car outside and read my email. Or, can I come in and sit at a table, order a glass of water, and then surf away on my laptop?

And what if the sign just says, "FREE WI-FI?" That's exactly what the sign at the Subway down the street from me says. Should I not take them at their word and log on from home if I can. (And I can!) After all, it says, "FREE Wi-Fi." Not, stop in and order something and use our FREE Internet while you're here. It says, "FREE Wi-Fi!" Same for the motel a little farther down the road. It doesn't say a thing about having to spend any money there.

In fact, if you've ever played any of the 'games' a lot of businesses sponsor, they usually say, "NO purchase necessary." You don't have to buy something in order to play or win. Is the FREE Wi-Fi from Subway based on these same rules? And are all Subways the same? Do they all play by the same rules because they are franchises…or are all franchises different?

The biggest problem is…there's usually not much to go on in determining if an Internet connection is FREE or not. You could ask…and I've done this…but most of the time, the people working there don't have the foggiest idea of what you're even talking about. So I tend to be as incognito and unobtrusive as I can. If the sign says, "FREE," I take them at their word and log on. I don't make a big deal out of it. I don't sit outside the establishment honking my horn, flashing my lights, or put a sign in my window that says, "I'M USING YOUR INTERNET!" If I happen to be a mile or two away, I do the same thing. I don't download anything illegal and I try to use the business connection after the business closes. The main thing is…I don't do anything to call attention to myself.

If they advertise FREE Internet…I take them at their word, but I don't abuse the connection. Why should I? There are dozens of these types of connections even in my small town. Why not share them? Why make a nuisance of myself? I like the aspect of FREE Internet. I don't want to bite the hand that's feeding me.

When I scan my neighborhood to find out who's broadcasting WI-FI around me, 30 to 40 APs show up. Usually, about 25% of them will be open. These will have SSID names like, Linksys, Bill's router, Gray family, etc. These are individual's home APs. They are not usually intended to be 'free' APs even though they might be 'open.'

It's easy to tell these APs from the business APs. In the case of the Subway down the street, their SSID name is, SUBWAY. So it would be hard to miss that. In the case of the Vincennes downtown and park Internet APs, BridgeMaxx is providing the FREE service and as soon as you log onto the system it says that you're on the Brigemaxx FREE Internet system. Again, there's no doubt. Same with McDonalds, Motel 8, and the Ice Cream shop. These places have a banner ad that pops up when you get online. The FREE Internet they're providing is advertising for them and I imagine they write off the cost of the equipment and the service.

When I first logged on to the new "park" Internet service, it stated, "Welcome to Vincennes Park and Recreation's FREE

Internet service. Provided by Bridgemaxx." The key word again is, "FREE."

It's the other 20 to 30 'open' connections close to my house that I wonder about. Are these people just not savvy enough to turn on the router's encryption or do they just not care? I've talked to a lot of people who really do leave their connection 'open' just so others will have a way to get online. That's really nice of them, but it's dangerous too. Very bad things can happen when you do that.

The problem is that when you leave your AP unencrypted, you don't know what kind of access the people using it are making. Are they downloading music files? Are they visiting porn sites? Are they hacking into other computers using your Internet connection in case it gets traced back to them? Which in this case…means back to YOU! Are they terrorists? Who knows what they're doing. The problem is, they're doing it on your Internet connection. And if you left it wide-open, then you're responsible for what happens.

In the last chapter, I'll show you how to setup your home router so you won't have this problem. It's not hard to protect yourself. Just be aware that leaving your AP open, means anyone who can access it can pretty much do whatever they want. And it will all come back to your account.

For now, let's move on to "how" you can build some of these special antennas and see if you have any FREE APs nearby that you can log onto!

A Simple WI-FI Reflector

Many times you won't need to get the maximum distance out of an antenna to reach a free AP. This first project isn't really an antenna at all; it's a reflector. It improves the radiating power of a WI-FI antenna. If you live near a FREE AP, this may be all you'll need to reach it. But it has several other uses as well that I'll cover later.

As far as building, it's about as simple as it gets. It's a remarkable performer considering it only costs about a dime! Here's the parts list:

Parts List:
1. Piece of cardboard, 8.5 x 11 is fine
2. Aluminum foil
3. Glue
4. Styrofoam. A piece about an inch thick is best, but anything that will hold a curve will work.
5. Five or six safety pins

This is almost too easy. It's hard to believe that such a simple device can make so much difference. What we're going to do is to make a parabolic reflector that will focus the signal being transmitted by a remote AP onto a USB Internet Adapter. This adapter will connect our computer to the Internet. These adapters can be purchased at Walmart, or any electronics store that carries computers for around $30.00. Or, they can be found on eBay starting around $10.00. I like the Belkin USB adapters because they are easy to modify, though we won't need to modify it for this application.

Here's how it works. Most APs are omnidirectional. This means that the signal radiates equally in all directions. Our USB adapter is also omnidirectional. That's not what we want. We want it to be unidirectional. The power of our antenna is greatly increased when we modify it to receive in one direction only. The parabolic reflector we're going to build helps to accomplish this. Basically, it's just a curved piece of cardboard, covered with a piece of aluminum foil that collects and bounces the incoming WI-FI signals so they all meet at a single point.

It works in much the same way as a flashlight. Think of a street light. The light shines in all directions, equally as bright at any point. Now, think of a flashlight. It throws a beam of light in a single direction. It does this because a reflector behind the bulb gathers the light going to the rear of the flashlight, and directs it towards the front. Because the light is focused in one direction, it's many times brighter than it would be if it were radiating in all directions. This is the same principle behind our WI-FI reflector.

The size of the reflector determines how much additional signal we'll receive and the amount of curvature is computed to bring the signal into focus on the antenna built into the USB adapter.

It wouldn't do us any good to just be able to receive the remote signal if we couldn't 'talk' back to it. The issue is resolved because the reflector amplifies our transmissions as well. Just like the reflector on the flashlight. The power that would normally be wasted by sending our signal to the sides and rear is re-directed towards the AP we're trying to log onto. The reflector works in both directions and without modifying anything or voiding any warranties.

Most of my clients use this type of reflector to get greater coverage in their own homes, rather than to reach out to a distant router. (AP)

Building The Reflector

Other than tracking down a piece of Styrofoam, the only thing hard about building this reflector is in getting the correct curve in the design. I have a sample of the curve on my website http://www.randybenjamin.com/curve.jpg that you can print and use as a template.

Here's what I meant when I said most of my clients use this type of reflector to get greater home coverage with their own wireless router. In this example, think of the numbers on a clock. Your router is placed in the living room (2 o'clock position) and you need to reach computers in the bedroom and kitchen. On a clock they might be represented at 6 and 10 o'clock. If you widen the curve on the reflector, you'll get less power, but a wider reflection of the signal. Without the reflector, you may have only been able to pick up the router on just one of the computers. Since you're directing the power to where you want it, both of the computers can connect to the Internet.

Here's another example...suppose you were trying to reach a friend two houses away at the 9 o'clock position. This time, you only have a single computer you're trying to make contact with so you'll want to maximize the signal and reduce its spread. The curve on my template will do this nicely. Just aim the reflector towards 9 o'clock and the majority of the power will be 'beamed' in that direction.

This design isn't meant for long distance communications. It's mostly used to make sure your router can reach anywhere in your own house and yard. As with all antennas, the range is greatly affected by where the antenna is located. If it's inside a trailer, that's NOT good! The metal walls will block the signal. A brick wall isn't good either. As long as your goal is to connect to computers inside of your home, the brick wall or even the metal on the outside of a trailer won't hurt you. The rule of thumb is…the fewer things your router's signal has to travel through, the more powerful the signal will be on the receiving end.

Several friends and I have a gaming network setup between our computers. One friend is about 1,200 feet away. This is well beyond the normal operating range of the average home router. However, I can log onto his computer using my laptop with no external antenna. This is accomplished by attaching a reflector to his router's antenna and aiming it in my direction. It works great and cost next to nothing!

Back to building the reflector…Styrofoam is easy to work with. You can cut it with a kitchen knife, but it might be a little hard to find. If so, substitute. All you need is to find something you can shape into the correct curve and attach a piece of cardboard too. Wood or plastic will work just as well though they are harder to shape.

I'll assume you're using Styrofoam. Take the template from my website, cut it out, and lay it over the Styrofoam. Now, draw an outline around the edges and cut the Styrofoam along the outline you just drew. You'll also notice a place marked "hole" on the template. This is where the reflector fits over the router's antenna. Make a hole in the Styrofoam at this point. It should look something like this sitting atop the router's antenna…

Now, take your cardboard, (this doesn't have to be heavy, something about the thickness of the cover of a paperback book is about right) and hold it against the curve you just cut in the Styrofoam. Put a mark on it so that it covers the curve completely. (Around 7") We are going to glue it to the Styrofoam in the last step.

Measure the height of your router's antenna and add an inch to the measurement. This will be the height of the cardboard reflector. Now, cut the cardboard to these dimensions.

Cardboard doesn't reflect microwaves. Here's where the aluminum foil comes in. Cut a piece of aluminum foil about a half inch larger than the cardboard square. Lay the cardboard flat on a table. Smear some glue (about any kind will do) over its surface and center the aluminum foil over it. Use the glue sparingly but cover the surface as completely as possible. I used contact cement. It doesn't take much to hold aluminum foil. You can make this surface either the inside or the outside of the reflector. Microwaves travel through the cardboard easily. Fold the extra foil over the back of the cardboard and lay it aside to dry.

Next, we want to mount the cardboard and foil to the Styrofoam. I usually mount it about an inch or two up from the bottom of the cardboard. Smear a little glue on the edge of the Styrofoam. The connection between the cardboard and the Styrofoam needs to be stronger than the one holding the foil, so use the glue liberally. To hold it in place while it dries, use the safety pins. Start at either end and center the cardboard on the Styrofoam. Then push a safety pin through the cardboard and into the Styrofoam. This will hold it. Remove the safety pins when it's dry. If you used something other than Styrofoam, you may have to find something else to hold the cardboard tight until it dries.

All you need to do now is to slip your new reflector over your router's antenna and you're finished. Aim it in the direction you are trying to reach and you'll see a huge improvement in the reflected signal.

That's it. You probably had the materials lying around the house and didn't spend a penny building this simple reflector. It's a cheap, easy solution to reaching out a few extra hundred feet. Here's a picture of the completed reflector with the aluminum foil backing.

FREE Internet   33

Building A High-Gain WI-FI Antenna

There are several designs we could chose from. These designs are not entirely my own. They are designs I've found on the Net that I've modified to suit my own purposes. You can find similar ones on the Internet if you do a Google search for "Wi-Fi mods, Wi-Fi booster, Wi-Fi Shootout" or just use anything to do with Wi-Fi and antenna. You'll be amazed at what will pop up.

How good are these DIY antennas? They're great. They'll work as good as or better than many commercial antennas costing $100 or more. Like I mentioned earlier, some are almost free.

Before we start this next project, here's something you might like to check out. Back in 2005, a new record was set for an unamplified Wi-Fi connection. The contest was held just outside of Las Vegas called, the Wi-Fi Shootout. The object of the contest was to see how far a working Wi-Fi connection could be established using unamplified, off the shelf routers connected to passive antenna systems. During the contest, a new world record was established of 125 miles!

In 2007, that record was broken. A group of Italian amateur radio operators set the new record at 188.9 miles! Later that year, a group from Berkeley University working with Ermanno Pietrosemoli established a wireless connection between El Aguila, Venezuela and Platillon Mountain. This shattered the previous record. The new record is now 237 miles! This record was established using standard Linksys WRT54 routers (available at Walmart) and special high-gain antennas. The link is so long, that one of the routers had to be placed high on the mountain to overcome the curvature of the earth. Wi-Fi is a line-of-sight media.

34 Randy Benjamin

Now we're not even dreaming of achieving anything like this with our antennas. I just wanted to show you what has been done…just using antenna technology. The best I've been able to do distance wise, was to linkup with a friend's computer about 9 miles away. I've never tried to get out any farther because I've never had a reason to try. This was just an experiment to see if it could be done. But under the right conditions, I'll bet I could increase this by a wide margin.

Two YAGI Antennas For Medium Range

Thee next two antennas are examples I built early on when experimenting in WI-FI designs. They are NOT the most powerful...or the easiest to build. I've included them because I learned a lot in making them, it was fun, and they did what I needed at the time. That said...for 99% of the people, I'd recommend the last two antenna projects, the **Dish***, and the* **WI-FI CANnon***. Theoe are the real powerhouses. You can build them in about a tenth the time it takes to build a YAGI antenna.*

The Yagi antenna has many uses. I'm calling it a medium range antenna, but with a few design modifications it could easily be included in the long range category as well. It's a lot harder to build than the simple parabolic reflector in the last chapter. The addition of a digital measuring caliper really simplifies things. I found one on eBay for $13.50 shipping included. When you are working in the gigahertz band, the elements in the antenna are very short; the longest is less than 3 inches. The digital caliper allowed me to measure the element lengths with a great degree of accuracy. I'm sure this greater accuracy also gave me better results. Using an old fashioned ruler and eyeballing it will work, but it's hard to achieve tenths of millimeter accuracy in this manner.

I like to use Yagi antennas when I want to reach out to a distance of up to a quarter mile or so. I can go a lot farther by adding additional elements but this complicates the building process and I can build a different type of antenna (WI-FI CANnon) much easier which will reach out even farther. This antenna can be as short as 13 inches so it's very portable. It fits nicely in my laptop case.

Here's a real life example of a Yagi antenna solving a networking and an Internet problem. One of my clients is a farmer who lives a little over 9 miles out in the country. He doesn't use the Internet much and has a dialup connection. One summer, he built a workshop about 1,300 feet from his house. It has an office in the loft and a repair shop on the first floor. He didn't think he'd need Internet in the office, but he did want to tie his home and office computers together so he could share files and work on his books from either location.

I suggested a wireless router to make the connection. A wireless router does more than just share the Internet. It's also the main component in setting up a network between two or more computers. The newest wireless routers operate at 100 mbps in the wireless mode, which is the same as most LAN (local area network) wired connections. So by putting a wireless router in his house and connecting a wireless USB adapter to his office computer, I could setup a network between the two. That is...if the wireless connection would reach that far, which it wouldn't...not without help anyway.

The maximum range of the most powerful router (the N series) is about 900 feet...and this depends on how many objects the signal will have to pass through.

In his case, we had a straight shot to the office but there were a couple of walls in the way. Our main problem was distance. We were well outside of the normal operating range of his router.

One thing we did have going for us was that we knew exactly where we needed the signal to go. This was a point-to-point connection that wouldn't change with time. All I needed to do was design a short, powerful, Yagi antenna to accomplish our goal. The Yagi antenna I designed sits on top of his home computer and is aimed at a cardboard/foil reflector attached to the USB adapter in his office. This setup works perfectly.

Once aligned, the two computers established a 100 mbps connection immediately. With the connection made, he could share printers, software, and most importantly, his data files. Now my client could work on his books from either computer. Because the computers were networked, he was also able to get on the Internet from the office computer. It was still a dog slow dialup connection, but since the home system was online, the networked office computer was online as well.

We talked about setting up a 'parabolic dish' antenna to see if he could hit one of the FREE APs in Vincennes, but no more than he was on the Net, he decided that it was probably more trouble than it was worth. He really wasn't very Internet savvy, but he was a hell of a farmer!

The key to the Yagi design is in having the software to figure out the lengths of the antenna elements, (made from stiff wire or paperclips) and the spacing between where they are mounted. You can find a design calculator that will give you the exact dimensions you'll need here: http://fermi.la.asu.edu/w9cf/yagipub/index.html. Just follow the instructions on the website to use the program. This program is an antenna modeler. You can get the correct dimensions for other frequencies as well. Use 2450 as the frequency for the Wi-Fi band. This is the center of the Wi-Fi spectrum.

One thing you need to be careful of when building the YAGI antenna is to use wire that's between 1 and 2 mm in diameter. This wire is used to make the elements that will direct the Wi-Fi signal into your computer. Wi-Fi operates in the gigahertz band. The frequency is so high that the wire's diameter makes a big difference in how well the antenna works. If you experiment with the antenna modeling program, you'll see what I mean. Also, make sure you have "Java" installed on your computer or the program won't work. You can find the Sun Micro version of Java here: http://www.java.com/en/download/index.jsp

Let's build this antenna. First, we need to decide how powerful we want to make it. Power equates to the number of 'director' elements in the design. Each director is a specific length aligned along a wooden dowel. Using the antenna modeler program, you can determine the power (rated in DB gain) for each configuration.

Why not just make the most powerful antenna and be done with it? That's not a bad idea except, the degree of difficulty in building the antenna grows as the number of elements increases…as does the antenna's size. That's the trade off.

The design I settled on used 12 elements and produced a little over 14 DB of gain. Gain is measured using a logarithmic scale. Every 3 DB of gain doubles the effective radiating power of the antenna. So if you started with 100 mW of power, a 3 DB gain would give you the equivalent of 200 mW. At 6 DB you double that again to 400 mW. A 14 DB gain gives you the equivalent of over 2.5 watts of power! This is 25 times the 100 mW you started with. This happens by taking all of the energy flowing into it and directing it into a narrow beam. The more elements in the system, the tighter the beam and the more power it radiates.

These antennas are highly directional, which is a good thing. This means that we are only going to be sending and receiving signals in the direction the antenna is pointing. If there happens to an AP right next door to you, you'll still pick it up, but for the most part, this antenna will ignore anything it's not directly pointing at. The more elements, the tighter this directionality becomes.

The antenna modeler program shows designs from 12 to 40 elements. As I said, the trade off is in the ease of building, verses the effective radiating power of the antenna. Wi-Fi frequency is so high, (2.4 gigahertz) and the elements so short, that fabricating them gets harder as additional elements are added. The difference in the lengths of the elements is critical to the performance of the antenna, as is the spacing between the elements.

On the 12 element design, the two shortest elements are the first and second directors at the front of the antenna. They are 49.6 and 49.2 mm respectively. That's a difference of only .4 mm between the two, not very much. Now you see why I purchased the digital caliper from eBay. With it, it's much easier to make the elements the exact length called for in the design.

The elements become longer as you near the back of the antenna. The last two elements are called the driver and reflector. The difference in length between these elements grows to over 3.4 mm.

The 12 element Yagi is not nearly as powerful as the 40 element version. The 40 element Yagi produces another 6 DB of gain, which more than quadruples the power of the 12 element design. But it's also over five feet long! The 12 element antenna is less than 13 inches. Even if you add an extra couple of inches to attach mounting hardware, it's still portable. For our purposes, the 12 element design will do just fine. Now, here's what you'll need to build it.

Parts List:

1. Stiff wire for the elements. The thickness should be between 1 and 2 mm. You can also use simple metal paper clips. The first Yagi I built was with paper clips and it worked fine. They were also easier to work with. Get the Jumbo clips if you decide to go this way. Each jumbo clip will make two elements.

Some clips are vinyl coated and that's OK too. The coating will help to protect the clips from corroding.

2. Square wood dowel. I got mine at Lowes in a length of 36 inch by 1/2 inch in diameter for $1.27. This will make two antennas.

3. Ruler that measures in millimeters and inches. (There are 25.4 mm per inch) You can find these at any office supply. I got mine for $1 at Walmart.

4. Wire ties…small size, around 3 or 4 inches long. Found these too at Walmart for $1.25.

5. One can of Polyurethane paint to protect everything from the weather. Two coats sprayed lightly over the entire antenna should provide plenty of protection. It won't hurt to get it on the antenna elements. If you are not using vinyl coated paperclips, you'll want to be sure the elements are coated as they tend to corrode if they get wet. Polyurethane paint is about $7 at Lowes.

Option A: An N-plug connector for connecting the antenna to the down lead antenna wire. (You'll only need this if you are using an internal Internet card for your Internet connection. This is how I connect my desktop computer.) Radio Shack has these for $4.99.

If you're using an N-plug connector, you'll also need a three or four foot length of LMR400 (or equivalent) antenna wire. This is special 'low loss' wire. It's about $2 a foot at Radio Shack. Again, you only need this if you are using an internal Internet card. To get the wire into your computer, you'll need a connector that matches your internal Internet card's input jack, another $5 dollars.

The easiest way to get these items is to purchase them already assembled. I found them for sale at Amazon.com and eBay for $20. This is everything, cable, N-plug, and card connector. Just tell them what internal Internet card you have (D-link, Belkin, Linksys, etc.) so they'll know which cable you'll need.

Option B: A Belkin USB wireless adapter is what you'll need if you're not already using an internal Internet card. I use this type of adapter for my laptop, even though it already has a built-in wireless networking card. They can be purchased on eBay for around $15. No N-connector or cables are needed if you use a USB adapter. You can use other adapter brands as well. I chose the Belkin because it's easy to modify and I already happened to have one!

Tools needed:
1. Drill with a 1/16" drill bit.
2. Wire cutting pliers.
3. Solder gun and solder.
4. Exacto knife with pointed blade to cut foil traces if using a USB connector.
5. Any kind of saw to cut the wood dowel.

Option: I used an electric grinding wheel to grind the antenna elements to the exact measurement needed, but a simple metal file will work too. The metal on a paper clip is so thin; it's really easy to shape it to the proper length.

The hardest thing about building this antenna is getting the element lengths and spacing as close to the design specs as possible. With the digital calipers, it's much easier. If you just plan on building one antenna, it's kind of foolish to go to the extra expense of buying a digital caliper.

Ok, if you've gathered the materials, let's build this puppy!

Element	Length	Position
1	59.61216	0.0
2	58.55396	18.34220
3	55.20298	25.74963
4	53.61567	39.50629
5	52.38110	58.55396
6	51.67563	82.18718
7	50.97016	109.70049
8	50.61743	140.74114
9	50.26469	174.60367
10	49.91196	210.93535
11	49.55922	249.38343
12	49.20649	289.59518

1. The first thing we'll need is a printout of the element lengths and spacing. When you run the antenna modeling program, it will produce these measurements. (Reproduced in the chart above.) Now, let's start by drilling the holes that will hold the antenna elements. Take the 1/2 X 32 inch square wood dowel and cut it into two 16 inch pieces. The extra 16 inch section can be used as a backup or to build a second antenna. We really only need about 12.5 inches to mount the elements, but the extra length will give us something to work with in case we decide to install mounting hardware.

2. Next, we're going to mark the distance between the elements on the dowel so we can drill the mounting holes. Look at the spacing chart. Let's start at the rear of the antenna with the reflector. Measuring from the end of the wood dowel, draw a line across the wood at 101 mm. There will be 12 elements in all and this is where the first one will be mounted.

This line will be used as a reference for all of the remaining elements. By using this line as a base, we won't be amplifying any errors as we continue to mark the positions for the other elements. All measuring will be done from this line.

3. Using the baseline as a reference, measure towards the front of the dowel and draw a line at these positions. 18.3 mm, 25.7 mm, 39.5 mm, 58.6 mm, 82.2 mm, 109.7 mm, 140.7 mm, 174.8 mm, 210.9 mm, 249.4 mm, and 289.6 mm. Try to draw this line as near to specifications as you can.

We want the elements to be located in the center of the dowel so, on the first line and the last, make a mark at 6.25 mm (center) position. Now, draw a line between these points. Where the lines cross is where we will mount the elements.

4. Drilling the holes for the elements is easier if you have access to a drill press. This assures a perfect 90 degree angle with the dowel and all the elements will line up perfectly. I've found that it's easier to drill dead center where the lines cross if you punch a guide hole first. The wood is soft. Something pointed, such as a small nail, or even a needle works just great. Just push it into the wood a millimeter or so and then move it in a circular motion so that it widens the hole just a bit. The trick is to have a place for the drill bit to fit into. Just a slight indentation is all it takes.

The size of the bit is important. I used a bit that was slightly larger than the size of the antenna elements. The paper clip was 1.5 mm, and I found a 1.7 mm bit in my toolbox. All of the elements are the same size, so you can drill all of the holes with the same bit.

If your hole is too large, you can always wrap a few windings of Scotch Tape around the element to hold it in place. Or, just put a drop of super glue on it. Try to make it as snug as possible though. Mine fit tightly but I still used a touch of glue to lock them in place. We'll paint everything with polyurethane paint later but for now, we're just interested in getting the holes drilled and the elements mounted.

5. Next, it's time for the hard part…making the elements. As I said earlier, you can use stiff wire or metal paper clips. You'll size both the same way…by grinding or filing them to the correct size. This sounds much harder than it is.

First, we'll need the chart showing the element lengths. Starting from the back, they are…59.6, 58.6, 55.2, 53.6, 52.4, 51.7, 51.0, 50.6, 50.3, 50.0, 49.6, and 49.2. These are very close measurements and the closer you can come to getting them the exact length, the better your antenna will work.

Here's a tip on getting the elements to the correct size. Always start with the longest element first. That way, if you happen to take too much metal off of the element, you can always size it to the dimensions of the next shorter one, then go back and make the one you were trying to make to begin with. The metal in a paperclip is really soft. It's easy to file it to the correct length with a fine tooth metal file. The grinding wheel makes short work of it though.

As you make each element, be sure to mark it so you'll know where it goes on the dowel. The lengths are so similar; it can be hard to tell them apart. I use a short piece of masking tape to keep from mixing them up. I lay the tape sticky side up on my desk, then place the element directly in the center of it and fold the two ends of the tape together. Then I write the element's number and size on the tape. This way, it's hard to get them confused.

6. Once you've drilled the holes and made the elements, it's time to mount them on the dowel. They need to be centered on the dowel. There's a little trick to this too. It's easy to find the center of each element. Just divide its length by two. The problem is...even if you mark the center, you can't see the mark once it's inserted into the hole in the dowel. What you really need is to mark the element so that when this mark touches the edge of the dowel it will be centered. To do this, divide the length of the element by two, then add 6.25 mm to it, (distance from the center of dowel to the edge) and make a mark there. Insert the element into the hole until it reaches this mark and the element will be exactly centered in the dowel.

Here is where you'll need to make a mark on the elements starting with the longest element (rear) first. Measure from the end of the element towards the center and make a mark here (longest first): 23.5, 23.0, 21.0, 20.5, 19.8, 19.5, 19.1, 19.0, 18.8, 18.6, 18.4, and 18.3. These measurements are extremely close. If you have a digital caliper, you can get it right on the money.

7. Now, we're going to mount the elements in the holes we drilled earlier, with one exception. Don't mount the "driven element" this is the second element from the rear. We have to do some things to it first. But we're ready to mount the others. You should have each element marked, so all you have to do is to push them into the correct hole in the dowel. Insert them until the centering mark you made just touches the dowel's edge. At this point, they should be centered. I like to add a drop of glue to each side once they're centered. Super glue works great.

I usually start at the front of the antenna and work my way back. Remember, the driven element (the second from the rear) needs some additional work done to it before it's ready to be installed. You can either cut all of the elements before you start installing them, or you can cut them one at a time installing each as soon as you've sized it. I've done it both ways and prefer installing them as I cut them. It's much easier to keep from getting them mixed up this way.

The 'driven' element requires a little more work than the straight director and reflector elements. I like to make it out of solid copper wire with no insulation. We're talking about a piece of wire a little over 5 inches in length so this shouldn't be too hard to find. Strip the insulation off of an insulated piece of wire if you don't have any bare wire to work with. Notice that the listing for the element sizes in our chart says the 'driven' element is only 58.6 mm, which is just a little over 2.4 inches…why did I say that we need a 5 inch wire for the element?

We have to double the size of the element because it's not just a straight piece of wire like the director and reflector elements. It folds back over itself. About a 5mm gap is needed between the top and bottom of the fold. So we're going to need a wire of about 130 mm or 5.1 inches in length to make the driven element.

The 'driven' element needs to be shaped in a pattern that resembles a paper clip. (See pics.) The easiest way to do this is to mark the center of the wire and then put a mark about 30 mm from each end. This will represent the outer edge of the bend in the paperclip. Use a pair of needle nose pliers to make the bend. It should be as round as possible with the mark you made in the center of the bend. Bend the wire so that it lays back over itself.

The end of the wire should stop just short of the center. Now, put the straight end of the wire through the hole in the dowel so that that top/end of the wire you just bent is just short of the center of the top of the wood dowel. You'll need to make an identical bend in the end you just passed through the dowel so that it matches the first bend. It will look much like a paper clip with the lower end passing through the dowel.

The idea is that we will attach either the N-plug, or the USB device to the ends of this wire. This is where the WI-FI signal is picked up and transferred to your computer. The 'directors' in front of the driven element, and the 'reflector' to the rear focus the incoming signals into this piece of wire.

Once you have the driven element made and inserted into the dowel, add a touch of glue to both ends to hold it in place.

If you are using an N-plug connector to attach the antenna to your computer, you'll need to connect it to the dowel next. The easiest way to do this is to use a wire tie and epoxy. The connector can be mounted with the 'tip' or positive pin almost touching the driven element. The 'tip' is isolated from the outer 'ground' of the connector. I try to get the 'tip' to within a few millimeters (1/4 inch at most) of the driven element. Then I can solder a short piece of wire from the tip to one end of the driven element.

The outer part of the N-plug is the ground. You'll need to solder a wire from it to the other end of the driven element.

Again, make the wire as short as possible. The back end of the N-plug is a screw-on connector that will accept the cable running to the internal Internet card in your computer. One cable tie and a spot or two of epoxy will hold the N-plug solidly to the wood dowel.

I'd guess that very few of you will be using internal Internet cards. So instead of the N-plug connector, you'll be using a standard USB adapter. These work great and they are much easier to use than the N-plug setup. Every computer has a USB connection on it. Most have four or more. The USB adapter we'll be modifying has a built in antenna that we'll need to disabled before it can be connected to our Yagi antenna. Since all of the DIY antennas except the 'reflector' can use this USB device, I've included a separate chapter on how to do this modification. It's the chapter called, **"Modifying The Belkin USB Adapter."** Once modified, you can attach the adapter to the antenna with a wire tie or Velcro.

Here's what the finished antenna will look like…

This is not the easiest antenna to build. There's a lot of detail in cutting the elements and getting them precisely aligned along the dowel. But it does have its advantages, especially because of its small size. It's a good performer for such a small package. The only problem I find with the YAGI design is that it requires a lot of work compared to the WI-FI CANnon which is much more powerful and can be built in about a tenth the time.

YAGI Loop Antenna

The YAGI loop antenna is a variation on the YAGI antenna we just built. This one is going to be a little more powerful because we're going to be using more elements. It's also 'physically' a little longer. I chose an 18 element design for this example.

Like the original yagi, I'm going to use the USB adapter to connect the antenna to your computer. If you have an internal Internet card, you can substitute an N-plug connection and save the cost of the USB adapter. By using the USB adapter, you can swap this antenna between computers easily. All computers have USB ports, while only a few have internal Internet cards.

The main reason that this antenna is more powerful is because we're using more elements. The more elements in your design, the higher the gain, and the tighter the transmit/receive pattern. So this antenna will be much more directional as well.

The other thing that improves the power is the much larger reflector at the rear of the antenna. We used a simple wire as the reflector for our first YAGI antenna. On this one, we're going to use a copper back-plate approximately 4 x 5 inches in size. You could also use a circular back-plate, but it's harder to cut and though it looks more high-tech…it doesn't really add any additional power over the square model.

Let's start with a parts list:

1. The loops can be made from either coated or bare, 'solid' copper wire. I didn't have any bare wire available but I did have some old Romex 3 lead house wire. It worked fine for the loops. If you have to buy wire, look on eBay. I found 10 foot lengths of bare 16 gauge copper wire selling for 60 cents per foot, shipping included. This heavy gauge wire will keep its loop shape better than a lighter gauge. Because of the high frequency of the WI-FI spectrum, we'll only need 6.5 feet of wire to build this antenna.

2. Copper tubing: Look for a tube that's twenty four inches in length and about a half inch in diameter. I found one in the plumbing section at Lowes for $3.87.

3. Copper clad PC board. This can be found at Radio Shack for about $4 including tax. It can be either solid copper coated or it can have tiny copper connection points (solder holes) on the surface. Either one will work fine. The holes are for connecting surface mount components. They won't affect the performance of the antenna. The only one in stock at the local Radio Shack was actually 4.5" by 6.25". The larger size is fine.

4. Belkin USB adapter. I chose Belkin because I happened to already have one and it's easy to modify. The best place to pick one up is on eBay, either new or used. I've seen them used for as little as $10. New, they run around $30 to $35.

5. Quarter inch barrel adapter to mount the copper tube to a camera tripod. The barrel adapter mates to the quarter inch bolt. That's standard on almost all camera tripods. You may need to ask someone at Lowes to help you find one. Just tell them what you want to do and they should be able to find one for you in no time. It has a female fitting on one end and a male on the other. I drilled a mounting hole in the copper tube a quarter inch back of center and threaded it for the barrel connector. In hind sight, I probably could have attached the tripod directly to this threaded hole and eliminated the barrel adapter.

6. Solder and soldering iron. A 25 watt iron is best for soldering to the USB adapter's circuit board. Pliers, wire strippers, and a small vice (for holding the tubing while attaching the elements) hot glue gun, pocket knife, and a small metal file will make things easier.

Making the Loops

Once you've gathered the parts, the first thing that needs to be done is to form the wire into the loops that will be used for the elements. Before you can do this, you'll need to know the dimensions of each loop. You can download a program on the Internet that will calculate the lengths of the loops depending on the frequency and number of elements you're working with. It's a DOS program, but it works well. You can download (save it) or run it directly from my website, here's the link: www.randybenjamin.com/yagi.exe

Some of you may not have worked in DOS (Disk Operating System) before. This is the environment we had to work with before Windows came out. It's not very user friendly but you'll only be using it for a few minutes to get your element dimensions.

When you 'run' the program, your screen will turn black and a small blue window will appear. You'll be asked for the frequency (2450) and the number of elements. (18) Enter these numbers and it will calculate the dimensions of each element. If you're building the 18 element antenna I'm using in this example, I've saved you the trouble of doing this…here's a chart showing the dimensions needed. If you decide to use more or less elements, you'll need to run this program to get the correct dimensions.

Here are the measurements for my 18 element design:

```
LOOP_Y~1.EXE

Label.              Circumference.      Cumulative
Reflector 1         74 by 61 mm.        0 mm.
Reflector 2         134 mm.             42 mm.
Driven              123 mm.             54 mm.
Director 1          114 mm.             69 mm.
Director 2          114 mm.             80 mm.
Director 3          114 mm.             105 mm.
Director 4          114 mm.             129 mm.
Director 5          114 mm.             145 mm.
Director 6          114 mm.             176 mm.
Director 7          114 mm.             224 mm.
Director 8          114 mm.             272 mm.
Director 9          114 mm.             320 mm.
Director 10         114 mm.             368 mm.
Director 11         114 mm.             415 mm.
Director 12         114 mm.             463 mm.
Director 13         110 mm.             511 mm.
Director 14         110 mm.             559 mm.
Director 15         110 mm.             607 mm.

Do you require hard copy of these values (Y/N)
```

As you can see, elements 13-15 are the same length, as are elements 1-12. There are several ways to form the loops. What I like to do is to measure the lengths I need and then make a mark on the wire where I want to cut it. Then I wrap the wire around something that is a tiny bit smaller than the loop I need. The heavy gauge wire holds this shape pretty well. I found a salt shaker that was just about perfect. With the wire tightly wrapped around it, I cut the loops at my marks one at a time.

Here's an example:

If you used coated wire, you should strip off about a quarter inch of insulation at both ends of the wire. Mount the wire so the bare wire touches the copper tube.

When you've finished cutting the wire for the elements, they should look something like this...

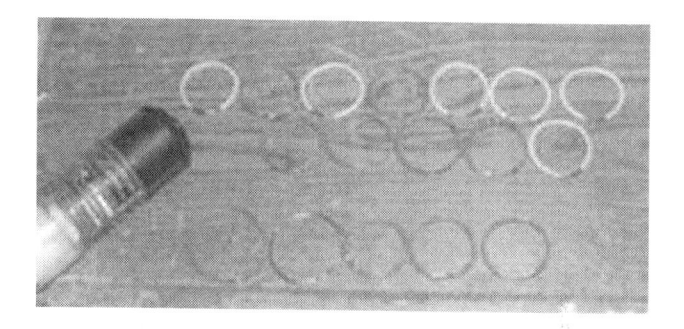

This was a lot easier than I expected it to be. The wire is stiff enough that it holds its shape very well. If it does lose its shape, it's no problem to bend it back like it should be.

Once the wire is shaped into loops, it's time to mark the copper tube. I started marking from the reflector end first. The same chart (above) that listed loop lengths also lists the positions where the loops need to be mounted along the copper tube.

The lengths are listed in millimeters. One inch equals 25.4 millimeters if you'd rather work in inches. But it's a lot easier to go ahead and use the metric scale for most of these measurements. Notice that the last director, number 15 is 607 mm from the square reflector at the other end of the tube. This is 23.9 inches. So the two foot tube is perfect for the 18 element design.

Once you've marked the tube, it's time to mount the elements. I used a vice to hold the tube while I mounted the elements. My first choice of mounting the loops was to solder the bare (the quarter inch of insulation we stripped off earlier) wire to the tube. But this takes a propane torch to get the copper tube hot enough to accept the solder, which I didn't have. I decided to epoxy them to the tube instead. This presented another problem. You need to have a good electrical connection between the loops and the tube and regular epoxy doesn't conduct electricity. What I needed was conducting epoxy.

Conducting epoxy can be found on eBay but it's expensive. Fortunately, you can make your own by mixing 'graphite' into the epoxy as you use it. Graphite can be purchased at about any auto-parts store. Ask at the counter for the lubricating graphite used to condition door locks. It's about $5. One brand is **AGS Extra Fine Graphite** but I'm sure there are many others. I mix a very small amount of epoxy and then put enough graphite into it to turn it a light to medium gray. One tube of graphite/epoxy mix will be more than enough to attach the 18 elements.

Attach them one at a time. Quick setting epoxy will hold like solder and it's easy to work with. It just takes a couple of drops to hold the loop tightly on the copper tube. Just mix enough for two connections at a time as it sets very quickly.

Attach all of the loops to the tube except the driven element and the square (base) reflector. This is the copper clad PC board you got at Radio Shack. We need to drill two holes in the PC board. First, find the center of the board by drawing a line between the two diagonal corners. Where they cross is the center. We're going to be using this point as a reference to work from..

Using the center as a base point, we're going to drill a hole the same size as the outside diameter of the copper tube. You can drill it slightly smaller if you like, and then ream it out. We need the center of this hole to be 26 mm directly under the center of the reflector. This is where the tube will connect to the reflector. We also need to connect the USB adapter to the driven element. To do this, we need to mount the USB adapter just under the top and inside of the loops. Make another mark

18mm above the center of the reflector. This is where the USB adapter will be mounted. Refer to the drawing below to visualize what we're doing.

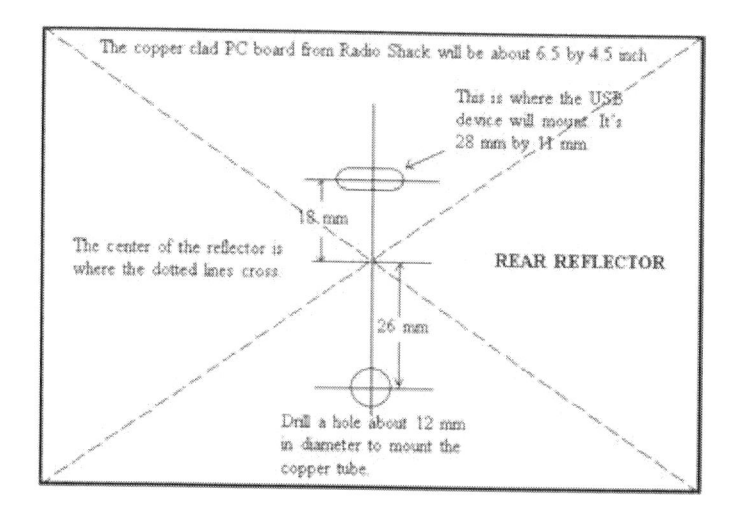

```
The copper clad PC board from Radio Shack will be about 6.5 by 4.5 inch

                            This is where the USB
                            device will mount. It's
                            28 mm by 11 mm

                    18 mm
The center of the reflector is
where the dotted lines cross.          REAR REFLECTOR

                    26 mm

            Drill a hole about 12 mm
            in diameter to mount the
            copper tube.
```

Now, we need to modify this last hole so that it matches the shape of the adapter. The Belkin adapter is 11 mm at its thickest point and 28 mm wide. I used a fine point Sharpie ink pin and drew the outline of the adapter on the reflector. Then I took an 11 mm drill bit and drilled a hole at the center of my outline. Then another to the right and left of center until I had most of the material removed in the outline of the adapter. I was able to clean it up and shape it perfectly using a small metal file. If it's not a tight fit, don't worry about it. We are going to use a few drops of 'hot glue' or epoxy to hold it in place after we modify the adapter.

Once the adapter fits snuggly into place we are almost done with the tube assembly. It's time to make the driven element. The driven element is shaped differently than the directors. While the other elements were, "closed' loops, the driven element will be left open. These open ends will attach to the USB adapter's antenna connection.

This wire is easier to work with if it's bare copper. I used Romex (house wiring) so I had to strip the insulation off before I could attach it. No big deal. You can use wire strippers or even a sharp knife. We want to shape this wire into a loop just like the others, but instead of attaching it to the tube where the ends meet; we'll attach it so these ends are on the top of the loop and not touching. Find your mark on the tube for the driven element and epoxy it to the mark just as you did with the other loops. The open ends will be at the top.

When we actually mount the USB adapter in place, it will only be a few millimeters from these ends and we'll run wires attaching each end to the USB adapter. Once the epoxy dries, spread the loop so that the ends of the wire are 4 or 5 mm apart. That completes the tube assembly. It's time to modify the Belkin USB adapter.

Modifying The Belkin USB Adapter

This next part takes a steady hand and a little soldering expertise. If you've never soldered before, this might be a little intimidating. Ask around and see if one of your friends knows how to solder. We are going to be soldering wires to a very tiny spot on the circuit board. There are four solder connections we'll be making. The two on the circuit board require a low wattage soldering iron. A 25 watt iron is perfect. The other two connections are on the driven element. These are easy to make and heat will not be a problem.

Here's how we do the modification. The first thing we need to do is to take the plastic cover apart. A small flat screwdriver or a pocket knife is all you'll need. I used a pocket knife. Just put the blade in the seam running along the edge of the adapter and pry the two sides apart. Start at one end, pry it up about 1/16 of an inch, then move the blade up a half inch or so and pry again. Once you get it started, the two halves will come apart easily.

This will reveal the adapter's circuit board. It should look like this. We'll be working on the circuit board to the right of the aluminum shielding. We're going to cut the connections to the internal antenna, and attach two wires leading to the driven element on our loop antenna.

60   Randy Benjamin

The best tool to use to cut the connection is an Exacto knife. You can find one at any hobby shop or office supply store. There are two pictures that follow. The first one is a close-up of the area we'll be working on before we make the cut.

We're going to cut the trace between C11 and C152. Next, we'll scrap off the green paint until we can see the aluminum foil underneath. This will be just to the right of where we made the cut in the traces. They are marked, 'cut' and '<scratch' on the picture on the next page.

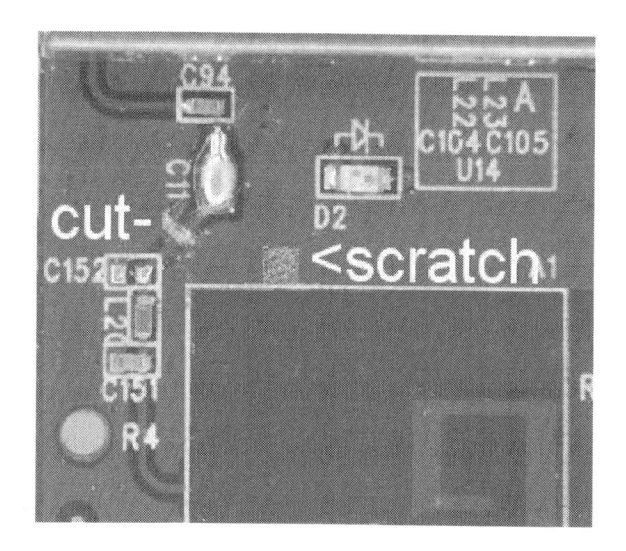

Use the antenna to keep everything oriented in the right direction. It's the square shape just under the '<scratch' on the diagram.

Now comes the touchy soldering part! We'll need two pieces of insulated wire, 2 inches in length with about an 1/8 of an inch of the insulation stripped away from the end. Wire from 18 to 20 gauge works best. It can be stranded or solid. One of these wires will be soldered to the connection at C11 and the other to the foil we uncovered when we scratched the green covering off of the circuit board. The C11 connection is the most heat sensitive. The best way to do this is to pre-tin one end of each wire with a little solder. You can also heat the foil with the tip of the iron, and touch a bit of solder to it. You are really just letting a drop of solder melt on the tip of the soldering iron then touching this drop to the foil. It should stick when it touches it.

These wires will extend outside the USB case and attach to the driven element on our antenna. I made these wires longer than necessary at 2 inches. We will be cutting them down once we have the device mounted.

Once soldered in place the wire needs to pass through the end of the plastic case. All you need here is an opening large enough for the wire to fit through. I used the edge of a small metal file to make a notch in the plastic. It's very soft and easy to shape. I notched the bottom part of the case just under the seam.

OK, let's solder the wires. The hardest one is the C11 connection. Align the wire so that it's facing towards the end of the device where you notched the case. Take the end of the pre-tined wire and hold it against the C11 connection. Touch the soldering iron to it until it melts. This will only take a few seconds. Pull back the soldering iron but hold the wire in place for another 15 to 20 seconds…or until the solder hardens. Blowing on the connection always seems to help. This really isn't that hard if you've done any soldering at all.

Now we'll do the same thing with the other wire touching it to the aluminum foil we uncovered. Again, if you've pre-tined both the foil and the wire, just a touch of the soldering iron should be enough to liquefy the solder and make the connection. Be sure it's aligned towards the notch you cut in the plastic as well.

Once you've made the solder connections, you can put a drop of hot-glue, epoxy, or super glue on the wires to hold them in place. There's a perfect spot just between the circuit board and the notch. With this done, you're ready to snap the case covers back together.

We want as short a connection as possible between the driven element and the USB device. Push the USB case through the mounting slot you made in the square reflector. It should go right up to the driven element. The wires will most likely be a little long so cut them back to where there's just enough wire showing to make a connection to each end of the driven element. You'll need to strip off about 1/8 inch of insulation after cutting the wires. Pre-tin both the wires and the ends of the driven element. The driven element is much heavier wire so you'll have to apply more heat this time. That's OK because there aren't any electronic components near the solder points. Attach one of the wires to the right end of the driven element, and the other one to the left end.

Once this is done, apply a few drops of hot-glue to the case where it goes through the slot in the rear reflector. That's all you need to hold it securely in place.

We're done. The finished antenna should look something like this.

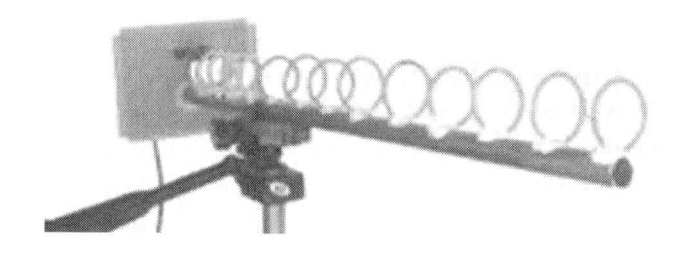

All that's left to do now is to install the Belkin adapter's software, attach the antenna to a camera tripod, (shown) and start looking for those FREE WI-FI connections.

Now For The BEST!
The Parabolic Satellite Dish And
The WI-FI CANnon

OK, I've saved the best for last. The next two antennas are EASY to build, whereas the YAGI designs were medium to hard. This is where things get interesting.

The parabolic satellite dish antenna is one of the most powerful (by far) WI-FI antennas you can build. This is the one that I use in combination with the next antenna design, the WI-FI CANnon. Not only is it powerful, but you can build it in about ten minutes!

How expensive it is depends on where you find the satellite dish. I'm talking about one of those small (18 to 30 inch) dishes such as a DISH network or Direct TV dish. Not the old 'huge' satellite dishes. If you look around, you may well be able to find one for free. When people drop satellite service and go to cable, the satellite company hardly ever takes the dish back, only the LNA at the focal point. Many times they don't even bother with that. Ask around, you might snag onto one of these dishes for free. I see them in yard sales all the time for $5 or less. Offer a $1. You'll probably get it.

If you can't find one nearby, then look on eBay. I'm looking right now and there's a listing (8 available) for a brand new Direct TV dish with mounting hardware for $8.99 plus $9.00 for UPS ground shipping. That's about $18. This is the best price I found (I only looked at about 50 of over 1,600 listings.) but several others were listed for less than $30.00 shipping included. Shipping is usually more than the cost of the dish. If local pickup is available, and you're close...the dish by itself is usually less than $10.00. Be sure to check several listings. As is usually the case on eBay, some people will have the same exact item priced at double what other people do. So do a little searching and don't just take the first price you see.

While I was at it, I looked up the Belkin wireless USB adapter. It's been about two weeks since I last looked. The best price I found for a new one was $12.50. ('buy it now' with shipping included) I found one used adapter for $9.50 including shipping.

The USB adapter comes with a three foot cable. This might be all you'll need. If you decide to mount the dish on an outside wall or up on the roof, then you'll need a much longer cable. I found cables in all lengths on eBay. The one I'd probably get is a 16 foot cable for $5.99 shipping included. That was a 'buy it now' price too. My dish is mounted on the wall right next to my window. I got by on an 8 foot cable. The USB standard for cable lengths is 16' 5" without a booster. So try to keep your connections in this range.

This is all the hardware you'll need to build this antenna and there's hardly any work in putting it together. Total cost, even if you have to purchase everything…about $36.00. That's for the disk, USB adapter, and cable on eBay.

What Parts Will We Need?

Here's the nice part. You won't need to mess with cutting elements to precise dimensions. There are no elements. So there's no need for paperclips either. And you won't have to go to the hardware store to buy wood dowels, paint or glue. You won't need graphite. You won't have to mix any special epoxy concoctions. No solder gun is required because there's no need to modify the USB adapter. We're going to be using the dish to focus the remote WI-FI signal directly onto the USB adapter's built in fractal antenna. Forget the N-plug, this is much easier. No rulers or calipers needed either.

Remember when I said, "This is going to be easy?" Well let me say it again. This is one of the most powerful antennas you can build, and it's also the easiest! You'll need a screwdriver. That's about it. Depending on how and where you mount the USB adapter, you might also want some Velcro, or a few wire ties. And if it's going to be out in the weather, a small plastic or glass jar will come in handy…something just big enough to hold the USB adapter. You don't want it getting wet.

I left the best antennas for last, because I wanted to give you a few other options. This antenna is so easy to build and it's so powerful. If I'd have put it first, you'd probably never have gotten to the others. Actually, this one is so superior; it's really a no-brainer.

The main thing you'll need to think about is…where to mount it and how big of a dish you should get. I'm using an 18" DISH Networks dish. I've seen some dishes as large as 30 inches. I'd guess that these are more than double, maybe even triple the power of my dish. But mine is so powerful, and it was free, I don't think it would have been worth it to have gone to the trouble of finding a larger dish. Now, that said…if you live way out in the country and need all the power you can muster, then you should consider getting the largest dish you can find. But remember, it's going to be more expensive, harder to mount, and the elements (wind, snow, etc.) will play more havoc with it. So…if you don't need that extra power, a smaller dish should do just fine.

Another nice thing about the 18" dish is that it can be mounted on a camera tripod. I have a friend that likes to take his dish with him when he goes camping. By using the camera tripod, he can easily set it up in his tent, and aim it in any direction. The whole thing only weighs a few pounds. He uses it with his laptop and it works wonderfully.

FREE Internet

Here's our parts list:

1. Satellite Dish- 18 to 30 inch…about $18.00 on eBay, free or under $5 at a yard sale.
2. USB Internet adapter- I like the Belkin, but since we won't be modifying the device, any USB Internet adapter will work just fine. Just get the most reasonably priced adapter you can find. $15.00 tops on eBay.
3. USB extension cable- the length depends on how far away your antenna will be from your computer. You can find them on eBay from 6 to 16 feet. A 16 foot cable is $6.00. A three foot cable is included.
4. Small plastic or glass jar- To hold the USB adapter and protect it from getting wet. (Most likely free.)
5. Velcro or wire ties- These are used to hold the USB device to the LNA support on the dish. ($2 to $3)

Let's Build It

Let's start with the dish. Depending on where you found it, it may or may not have the LNA (low noise amplifier) attached to it. The LNA is located at the focal point of the dish. It's on the end of the arm facing the front of the dish. Here's an example.

The dish shown has a triple LNA setup. The three LNAs are to the right on the picture on top of the bar extending from the bottom of the dish. Most likely, your dish will only have one LNA. This is where we'll attach our USB adapter. Before we do this, lets download some software that will help us to both locate surrounding APs and show us the best place to mount the adapter to the dish.

There are several programs we could use to measure WI-FI signal strength, but one of the best and easiest to use is called, WIFI-Sniffer. You can download it for free here: http://www.packet-sniffer.net/wi-fi-sniffer.htm

This software will display all of the wireless networks in your area. It shows the network SSID, its signal strength, the average signal strength over time, whether the AP is encrypted or not, and what type of encryption is being used if it is. It also shows the Mac address and channel the AP is operating on. That's a lot of useful information.

I use the signal strength meter to position the antenna so that it's pointing directly at the AP I'm logging onto. These antennas are very directional so it's critical to aim them accurately.

The software is also useful in finding the exact focal point of the dish. The LNA that comes with the dish is usually located near the focus of the dish. Though on some setups, there's a feed horn that helps to focus the arriving microwaves. The LNA is attached to a bracket that holds it in the prime focus by one nut and bolt. If you really want to find the exact focus, you can remove the LNA by taking out this bolt. Then you'll have to remove the LNA itself from the bracket holding it. This may be easy, or it might be a pain in the butt. It just depends on how lucky you are.

What we want to do is to place the USB adapter's antenna as near the exact focal point of the dish as we can. Before you remove the LNA, tape the USB adapter to it. Now bring up the WIFI Sniffer program and write down the signal strength of a couple of APs near you. Next, move the adapter to different locations near the LNA's focal point and take more readings. Take readings from several locations and see if there's much of a difference. You may find that you are getting higher (stronger) readings at points outside of the position of the LNA. Actually, the design of the parabolic dish is so overpowering that you can most likely just attach the USB adapter to the LNA without removing it. But if you do get a stronger signal somewhere else, you'll probably want to go ahead and remove the LNA and mount the USB adapter at the better location.

Either way, remember to incase the adapter in a small plastic or glass container. Both of my dishes are under the carport next to a window. They are pretty much protected from the elements. One of the dishes just has a plastic sandwich baggy over the USB adapter. I used a wire tie to attach it to the LNA. It was a ten minute setup.

Since I couldn't see my desktop computer (It was inside the house.) when I was ready to align my dish, I took my laptop outside and connected it to the antenna. I brought up the WIFI-Sniffer program and aimed my dish in the general direction of the nearest FREE hotspot. When its SSID showed up on the Sniffer's display, I knew I was close. Next, I adjusted the dish both horizontally and vertically in small increments watching the signal strength meter on WIFI Sniffer to see what difference it made. When I got the highest reading, I tightened the two bolts on the dish's mounting to lock it in place. The whole process took about 15 minutes.

Once I had the FREE AP dialed in, I removed the USB cable from my laptop, ran it over the window sill, and connected it to my desktop computer. To keep from damaging the wire, I made a small notch in the window sill so it didn't smash the wire when I closed the window. I was able to get by on an 8 foot USB cable.

When I first ran the WIFI Sniffer program, 11 APs showed up. Eight were encrypted and three were open. One of these was free. (Subway) When I was searching for the FREE AP that the city provides, 17 APs showed up. Every time I'd move the dish a few degrees, I'd lose some APs while new ones would appear. I live in town, so there are dozens of Wireless APs in my neighborhood.

This is such an easy antenna to build, you'll probably have it built and aligned in an hour or less. There's really not much to it. If you decide to go for the gusto and remove the LNA in order to find the perfect focus, you might add another hour to the project. But I doubt that will even be necessary.

The only hard part in building this antenna is in fitting the USB adapter inside of a protective device and then mounting it to the antenna. This is just something you'll have to experiment with. It will depend mostly on what you can find around the house to use as a holder.

In the two pictures that follow, you'll see that I removed the LNA and then wire tied the USB adapter to the bracket on the dish. This worked just fine and couldn't have been any easier.

FREE Internet 71

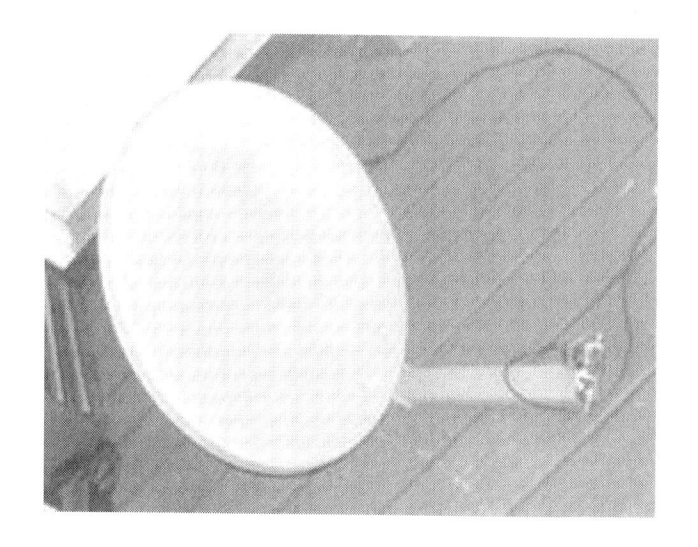

WI-FI CANnon (my favorite)

This antenna was originally designed to work in conjunction with the satellite dish as a way to better illuminate the dish. By illuminate, I mean it gathers the microwaves that are not at the prime focus of the dish and combines them with those that are. The more signal reaching the antenna, the more powerful it becomes.

The WI-FI CANnon is based on the one of the earliest WI-FI designs, the cantenna. Most of those designs used an N-plug connector and were a bit of a pain to build. The addition of the feed horn doubles the CANnon's power. When I first began to field test this antenna, I was amazed at how powerful it was as a stand-alone antenna. I found that I could reach APs that I knew were over a miles away. I did have the advantage of living on a hill, but this was still quite an accomplishment. When it's combined with a satellite dish, the combination is simply awesome.

So, what do we need to build this monster of an antenna?

Parts list:
1. 4 inch can (see building instructions) $5.41
2. Reducer – found at Lowes 6" to 4" about $5.50
3. 4" hose clamp – Lowes $ .75
4. USB adapter - $15 on eBay (or less)
5. USB extension cable $6 on eBay
6. Hot glue or "L" bracket to hold USB adapter straight

Let's Build the WI-FI CANnon

This antenna is basically a wave guide (can) with a feed horn (reducer) attached. The wave guide collects the microwaves coming from the distant AP and bounces them around until they are absorbed by the USB adapter. The feed horn, because if its greater collecting area (6" verses 4") gathers even more microwaves and directs them into the wave guide.

There are several designs for this configuration on the Internet but they all work in basically the same way. The main differences between the designs were the type and size of the can. After running an analysis of the most popular designs, the 4 inch seemed to give the most constant gain. The addition of the feed horn made it the ultimate performer.

On the Net, the can was always a point of discussion. Actually, the bottom of the can is the problem. If you look at cans on a grocery shelf you'll find that the ends are rarely flat! Almost all of them have circular grooves on both ends. These help to strengthen the can. Unfortunately, these grooves tend to reflect the microwaves striking them in odd-ball directions. There is a can though that doesn't have these grooves…at least, not on its top. It has a lid instead, and it's flat.

The can I'm talking about holds candy wafers made by Pepperidge Farms. The candy is called Pirouette. It's also the perfect size, about 7" deep and 4" wide. It too has grooves on the bottom, but we're going to turn it around and make the bottom the top. Since the lid is flat, (no grooves) it will make a great surface for our wave guide's bottom. I put the can in an electric can-opener and opened it from the bottom. This new opening will be the front of our wave guide.

It's kind of an expensive can. ($5.41 at Walmart) But the pastry-like wafers are wonderful! So you get a snack and a wave guide at the same time!

For the feed horn, I went to Lowes and looked in the heating department. I was looking for heat ducts. This is the metal ductwork that transfers heat from a furnace to the heat registers.

I was looking for what's called a reducer. Reducers are used to connect two different sizes of heat ducts. I needed a 6" to 4" reducer. This reducer makes a perfect feed horn for our antenna. It was less than $6 and fit perfectly over the 4" Pirouette can. To hold it in place, I used a common screw on hose clamp.

Before assembling the two pieces, I decided that they would look a little more professional if I painted them. This also had the advantage of protecting them from the elements. I painted the Pirouette can gray, and the reducer black using Rust-Oleum paint. The items should be connected electrically as well as physically so I put a couple of short screws through both the lid and the reducer just to be sure that everything was making a good connection.

Mounting the USB adapter was the last thing I needed to do. The hole for the adapter needs to be cut into the can in an exact location. I used the millimeter scale on my ruler and made a mark 44 mm from the end of the can. (The lid) This is where the center of the hole should be. This distance is critical to the design of the antenna.

In order to cut the square hole, I used a Dermal Tool with a cutting wheel. It went through the soft metal of the Pirouette can like butter. I used the USB adapter as a template, laying it on the can and drawing an outline around it. The grinding/cutting wheel made quick work of getting the exact size I needed. I made it just large enough that the adapter fit snuggly into the hole. It you get it too big, don't worry. We're going to secure it with either epoxy or hot glue, and then add an "L" bracket to keep it parallel with the bottom. (Lid)

The USB adapter's internal antenna is located about 10 mm from the end of the adapter. The calculations call for the antenna to be inserted 31 mm into the can so I had to add another 10 mm to this number to take into account it's location in the adapter. I made a mark 41 mm down from the end of my USB adapter and then inserted the adapter into the hole I'd just cut, stopping at the line. At this point, I used my hot-glue gun and put a bead of glue around one side of the adapter making sure that the adapter was perpendicular to the can. In about 30 seconds, it cooled and I went ahead and ran the bead entirely around the adapter. This will form a good water-tight seal between the can and the adapter.

In order to waterproof the USB cable where it connects to the adapter, I wrapped it in electrical tape. I thought about coating the connection with hot glue and then applying the electrical tape but since I'd be using this under my carport, I decided it wouldn't be necessary. If you plan on putting your CANnon out in the weather, you should take extra precautions to keep it from getting wet.

To keep rain and insects out of the antenna, I took the plastic cover from a 6" coffee can and placed it over the feed horn. (Reducer) To make sure that microwaves would go through it, I put it over a cup of water and put it in the microwave oven. After a minute, the water got very hot while the cup was just warm. The microwaves were passing through the lid with no problem. The lid fit perfectly over the reducer. I went ahead and put half inch beads of hot-glue at the top, bottom, and sides of the plastic lid just to keep it in place. In hindsight, I probably should have run the bead around the entire lid.

To make sure the adapter didn't develop a tilt from perpendicular, I attached (hot-glue) a 1" wooden "L" bracket that I found in my junk drawer to the can and the adapter. This can be any "L" shaped bracket you might have available. I could also have used Velcro to hold it in place.

Next, I hot-glued the USB cable to the side of the can using about an inch of glue bead. This took the pressure off of the cable/adapter connection. I could have held it in place just as easily with a wire tie.

So, that's all there is to making the WI-FI CANnon. It's not as easy as just taping your USB adapter to the LNA of a satellite dish, but it really is an easy build. If I had the parts gathered, I'd say I could put one of these together in an hour or two. Of course, waiting for the paint to dry takes a little longer. Unless you already have a satellite dish, this is the way to go. It works so well that it would be my antenna of choice, even if it was the hardest antenna to build. Here's the WI-FI CANnon with a CD next to it so you can better judge its size.

FREE Internet

Here's a picture of the WI-FI CANnon sitting on top of my workbench computer. I'm aiming at a friend's house about 1,500 feet away. Several of us have a game network setup so we can play against each other. The network is rock solid. It's going through one wall in my house and four walls in his. I have the CANnon sitting in a holder made from a $3 plastic miter box I found at Big Lots. It just happened to fit perfectly, so I used it. I've found that most of the time I can find what I need just by scrounging for it around my house and workshop.

UPDATE!

The addition of the 6" to 4" reducer (feed horn) to the original Cantenna design produced about 3 db of extra gain. That 3 db doubled the power of the antenna. While I was at Lowes looking for the reducer, I happened to notice an 8" to 6" one as well. After building the WI-FI CANnon, I decided to go back and get the larger reducer to see if it would give me even more power. It did! I don't have the equipment to measure the actual gain in db, but I did run some signal strength tests on local APs in my neighborhood. This led me to a couple of conclusions. First, adding the additional reducer raised the average signal strength of by about 35%. Converting this to db, I'd say this added between 2 and 2.5 db of additional gain. When trying to log onto a distant AP, that extra gain might just make the difference between only "seeing" the AP, and establishing a reliable connection. The $7 cost of the second reducer is well worth the money.

Another thing I noticed was that the number of APs showing up had dropped to only 8. Before, if I left the signal strength meter running over night, say…12 to 15 hours, I'd pick up as many as 18 APs, though many of them were too weak to log onto. And none of these were FREE. By adding the extra reducer, I'm not seeing as many APs, but I'm getting a stronger signal on those I am seeing. That's because the wider area of the 8" reducer is capturing more signals, while at the same time, the increased over-all length of the antenna is making it much more directional. So I'm losing those APs that are a few degrees off center. This is fine, as I'm really just looking for that one FREE connection anyway.

If you need more power, you might want to consider adding this extra element to your antenna. The 8" to 6" reducer was $7.15 at Lowes. I also bought another hose clamp for 75 cents to hold it in place. The total cost with tax was just under $9.

When I first started thinking about this upgrade, I realized the extra reducer would add even more length to the antenna. (15 inches in its present configuration) Because of this, I thought it might be a little awkward to handle. With the new section mounted it's 21.5 inches long. I decided that a handle located at the balance point might be a good idea. So while I was at Lowes, I went to the hardware isle and found a small (5") handle that worked perfectly. It was $1.99 plus tax. The one I decided on uses a bolt and nut to hold the handle in place. Most use screws. It's really hard to tighten a screw from inside the antenna. There's no room for the screwdriver. Be sure to insert the bolt so that the nut is on the outside. Try to keep the bolt as flush with the inside wall of the antenna as you can.

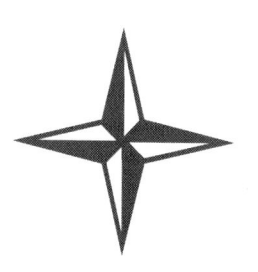

The Dish/WI-FI CANnon Combo

If you absolutely need the most power possible, combining the dish and the WI-FI CANnon will produce one of the most powerful antennas you can build or buy. Once you've built the CANnon, you only need to mount it to the dish. If you're going to make this combo, I don't think you'll need the extra reducer mentioned as an "upgrade" option. The Dish will supply all the signal we can handle.

Once I'd built the CANnon, I needed to mount it to the dish. The LNA that comes with the dish is located at the dish's focal point. So I needed to mount the CANnon's feed horn near this point. I removed the LNA by taking out the bolt that holds it to the dish. It's located on the arm coming from the bottom of the dish. I measured from the bolt, to where the LNA's wave guide was located. On my dish, this was 125 mm. The feed horn on the LNA extended forward 110 mm from this point.

This gave me a good starting point, but I was able to refine it even more by using the signal strength meter on the WI-FI Sniffer program. I aimed it at a nearby AP then moved it in/out and up/down recording the signal strength at each position. The position that gave me the best signal was where I wanted to mount the CANnon. It actually ended up being a little behind where the original LNA was mounted.

I didn't need the LNA but I did use the bracket holding it in place. I put the bracket in a vice and cut it so that the center of my CANnon would be located where the original wave guide on the LNA resided. I made a cut 50 mm from the center of the LNA. Next, I attached my CANnon to the bracket so that it was in the position I'd just discovered.

FREE Internet 81

These measurements might not work for you because your setup might be a little different than mine. You might have more than one LNA for instance or a dish of a different size. You should still be able to find the exact focal point though by using the same trial and error method I'm using. Once I found the 'sweet spot," I knew I'd be capturing nearly all of the microwaves reflecting off the dish's surface. Here's the cut I made in my LNA bracket. In the picture, the bottom part of the original LNA bracket is still attached to the arm coming from the antenna. One bolt holds it in place.

To attach the CANnon to the LNA bracket, I drilled a hole through the bracket and inserted a 4" bolt, leaving about an inch on each side to attach the tie-down cables. I used a nut on each side of the bracket to hold the bolt in place. (Shown in the picture above.)

At Lowes, I bought two short (6 inch) rubber tie-downs and attached them to each end of these bolts, then ran them up and over the CANnon and back to the bolt on the opposite side. There was just enough pressure to hold the CANnon tightly.

For a permanent mounting, a cradle could be made from 4" PVC pipe split into two pieces. One of these pieces could be mounted solidly to the LNA bracket. The CANnon could lay in the curve of this piece and be held in place by two hose clamps. I'm sure you can come up with other ideas but this one should work fine and at a cost of only a few dollars.

The reason the combination of the dish and the CANnon is so much more powerful than either device alone is because they compliment each other. With your USB adapter at the focal point of the dish, you're getting most but not all of the microwave energy. And it's nearly impossible to hit that point exactly. With the CANnon, you're getting nearly 100% of the waves reflecting off of the dish, even the ones coming in from off center. The feed horn has a wide mouth and gathers them together then shoots them down into the can where they bounce around and are absorbed by the adapter's antenna.

Because of the short distances between the sides of the can and the adapter's antenna, the waves don't fight each other. In the days when everyone used television antennas…this was a problem. Waves bouncing off of objects such as buildings would arrive at the television's receiver at different times and cause 'ghost' images to appear on the screen. WIFI wavelengths are so short, and the distances so minuscule, this doesn't happen. The waves just compliment each other and produce a stronger signal. If you really need the maximum distance obtainable, the dish/CANnon combo is about as good as it gets.

Here's a picture of the WI-FI CANnon used at the focal point of my satellite dish.

FREE Internet 83

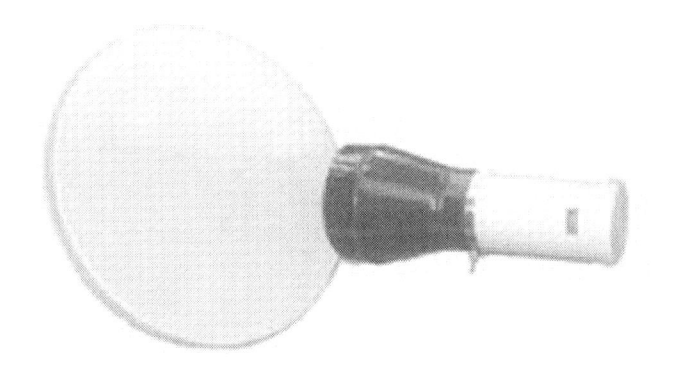

Keep Your Own AP From Being Compromised

Can you really keep someone out of your wireless network if they're determined to get into it? Probably not! But the good thing is…with just a few precautions, you can keep 99.99% of the people out.

Let's examine the situation realistically. The following discussion applies more to individuals than businesses, since a business has more reasons to be security cautious. Unless you're rich and famous, you're not likely to attract any 'dedicated' hackers. And that's who you'd most likely be dealing with if someone really wanted to 'hack' your AP.

Look at it this way. WEP and WAP encryption can be cracked, WEP in less than 10 minutes if the 'hacker' has the right tools. But why would someone want to go to the trouble of hacking your AP when there are so many 'open' APs to choose from?

Here's another way to look at it. Suppose a car thief decides it's time to steal his next car. He goes to a parking lot where dozens of nice cars are parked. Let's say he's only interested in cars worth 20 thousand dollars or more. He finds 15 that fit the profile. Of these 15, three of them have the keys in the ignition. He just narrowed his target from 15 to 3. What made the difference? The car keys of course. Why go through all the hassle of breaking into a locked car, pulling out the ignition and jumpering the wires when there are easier cars just sitting around waiting to be stolen. If he's a pro, it might only take him a minute or two to 'hotwire' the ignition, but why would he do this when he can just turn a key and drive away?

The same line of reasoning applies to your AP. If it's encrypted, why bother with cracking the encryption when there are so many unencrypted APs just sitting there for the taking.

And let's face it…if your AP is compromised, it's not likely to be by a hacker that did it. It's much more likely to be a neighbor! Though with one of these antennas, it might be a 'distant' neighbor.

Most people are just looking for a FREE Internet connection. They couldn't care less about who you are, or stealing your passwords, or reading your email. They're looking for FREE Internet access. Something as simple as turning on your router's encryption puts you in the "not worth the trouble category" when compared to those with wide-open connections.

It's hard for me to believe all of the unprotected APs I find in my own neighborhood. What's even more amazing is that in most cases someone actually went so far as to change the router's default SSID setting, but then didn't turn on the encryption. I see SSIDs like, "SMITH" or "Jones Family" or "Bill's Router" all the time so I know someone knew enough to change the router's default name. Why in the world didn't they turn on their encryption while they were at it?

I suspect that one of the reasons is that they couldn't get their laptop to recognize the AP with the encryption turned on. When you encrypt something (text, programs, or WIFI signals) you've got to follow the steps to unencrypt it exactly, or it won't work. Most problems are caused by not typing in the password correctly. Passwords are case sensitive. If you used a lower case letter when you made up your password, you've got to use that same lower case letter when you try to long on. Otherwise, it won't work!

Sometimes, using the wrong network 'group' is the problem. If your computer is using "workgroup" as the name of your network, then your laptop must be set to the same name or again…it won't work!

Encrypting your AP is extremely important. Even if it takes you a little extra time to get it right, it's worth it.

Here's how you can manually turn on your router's encryption. I'm using a Linksys router in this example, but Belkin, D-link, Netgear, etc., routers are all similar. To find the instruction for your particular router, log onto Google (http://www.google.com) and run a search using your router's name and model. If you have a Belkin router, typing something like this in the search box, "Belkin USB router setup" will get you what you're looking for.

Here's how to setup a Linksys router. Each model will be slightly different, but the general setup is the same across all models.

1. Bring up your browser and type this into the address field- http://192.168.1.1

This is the address of the ROM chip in the router. The address is hardwired. Some Linksys routers use- http://192.168.2.1 but most use the first address. When you type in this address, you'll be taken to the setup screen for the router. Here, you'll be asked for the login and password. The default login is usually "admin." (No quotes) If this doesn't work, just leave the login blank and go on to the password. The default password is also "admin". (All letters are in lower case)

2. Once you've entered the login and password, the main menu screen will appear. At the top of the screen you'll see "wireless" select this. From here you can change the SSID if you want, but the important thing is to click on the, "Wireless Security" tab. Several types of encryption will be shown.

3. Select the type of encryption you want to use. The safest is WAP. But you can choose any of the types listed. Both WEP and WAP will ask you for a passphrase. Use something you can remember easily, then click on "Generate" and several 'keys'

will be displayed. Write them down. These are the keys that you'll be asked for when you're ready to connect your laptop to the AP. Each key can be used with a different wireless device. These 'keys' are what protects your Internet connection from being accessed by anyone who is able to pick up your AP's signal. If they don't have the right key, they're locked out.

It's so simple to protect yourself. It's just amazing that everyone doesn't do it. Around my neighborhood, only about 25% of the APs are encrypted. I'd guess that's pretty true across all wireless communities.

It's really kind of stupid to leave yourself unprotected when it's so easy to turn on the encryption. After all, you wouldn't leave your keys in your car…why leave your AP open to the world?

I can be reached at: randy@randybenjamin.com. Kindle updates to this book are free from Amazon.com. Additional information can be found on my website at:

http://www..randybenjamin.com

Randy Benjamin

Randy Benjamin has been a computer technician for over 35 years. Before that, he was in the music business recording for several major labels. (Warner Bros, Curb, and Mercury Records) He also owned a small recording studio in the heart of "music row" in Nashville Tennessee.

In 1995, he began freelance writing, selling his first articles to Music Row Magazine. These articles were based around his experience as a computer expert and a working musician/singer/songwriter. They covered the electronic end of record production as well as the influence that the emerging Internet was beginning to have on the music industry.

In 1998 he started a newspaper column called, "The Internet Guide" that was syndicated in 23 newspapers. This column inspired two books, "The Internet Guide Handbook" and "More of the Internet Guide." Soon to follow was an interactive CD called, "The Healthy Computer."

In late 2008 he went back to his musical roots writing and producing a children's album and book called, "Tapestries." After demoing the album in Nashville, he decided that a one hour animated television special might be a possibility so he's currently pitching the idea to Warner Bros, Disney, and Hanna Barbara.

In September of 2009, he produced an album of original songs that's available on Amazon called, "Original Songs."

His first novel, a sci-fi thriller called, "Anomaly" will be released on Amazon in the summer of 2010.

Presently, he resides in his hometown of Vincennes, Indiana, living on a small lake with a dog named…Mufeoso.

Other books by Randy Benjamin on Amazon

Anomaly... (Summer 2020)

Anomaly is a 300+ page sci-fi thriller that will be released in the summer or fall of 2010. It chronicles the mysterious events that take place when the world's most powerful proton accelerator comes on-line. This isn't just science fiction; we're knocking on the door of this technology right now! Anomaly will be available in Kindle (ebook) and paperback versions.

Publish Anything On Amazon's Kindle...

This book is a guide for anyone wanting to know how to publish a Kindle ebook using Amazon's "Digital Text Platform." It also covers the usual...copyrights, ISBN numbers, pricing, websites, and everything else you'll need to get your book on-line and For-Sale at Amazon. The book is available in Kindle and paperback formats.

How To Transfer Cassettes To CD...

Having been a computer technician for 35 years, this is a question I'm asked over and over again. This ebook explains in detail exactly what you need to do in order to transfer cassette tapes to your computer so you can later burn them to a CD. It also includes the equipment necessary, (minimal) where to get it, and how much it will cost. This book is only available as a Kindle ebook.

"Original Songs" CD...

Before I started writing books, I was a songwriter. In my younger years, I was an artist/writer for several record labels in Hollywood including to majors, Mercury and Warner Bros.

I've been involved in music in one aspect or another, my entire life. Original Songs is an album I released on Amazon to showcase some of my best material. You can listen to samples on Amazon's website. Longer samples are available on my own website: http://www.randybenjamin.com.

-Summer of 2010-

Anomaly

By Randy Benjamin

Prologue...

The first sign that something wasn't quite right came a few days before Christmas, sometime around the 22nd if memory serves me. Most of the scientists and their families had already left for the holidays. Winter came early to Illinois. Frost whitened the landscape long before the sounds of "Trick or Treat" echoed throughout the countryside. In a cluster of brightly colored buildings, more reminiscent of Disneyland than that of the world's center for particle physics, a most astonishing discovery was about to take place. Questions that had eluded theologians and theoreticians alike were about to be resolved.

This discovery might just as easily have been made at Cal-Tech, or Stanford, or any of the prestigious European Universities. The Japanese had been at the forefront for years. The Russians too were searching for the Rosetta Stone, the skeleton key that would unlock the secrets of creation- secrets that until now had belonged to the Almighty alone. Even so, it seemed almost predestined that this discovery would take place in the United States. After all, the world's most powerful proton accelerator, Fermilab's super-conducting synchrotron, was located there. Nicknamed the Tevatron; keys that would unlock the secrets of the universe were patiently being forged deep within its womb.

Prominent scientists in the fields of quantum mechanics and cosmology had been coaxed from their respective universities to work solely on this project. They came from all over: Steven Tyco from the CERN Laboratory for Particle Physics near Geneva, Maxwell Bruiner from the DESY Institute in Hamburg, William Scott from the "Brain Trust" at Stanford's Linear Accelerator in Palo Alto. Even Professor Yamamoto, now in his 80's, the founder of Japan's famed Fifth Generation AI Lab, had seen fit to join this hallowed assemblage. After years of research and over a billion dollars in funding, the triumph these men so diligently sought was finally at hand.

Why was Tim Collins associated with such intellectual giants? Probably because his article "In Search of the Illusive Monopole" had won last years' coveted Pillanger award. Nova's turning it into a PBS documentary hadn't hurt either. In any event, as the science editor for *Future Technology* magazine, it was going to be his job to chronicle the discoveries taking place at Fermilab as they unfolded.

He would bear witness to nature's hidden wonders, observing the obliteration of protons, as they smashed into their component particles- quarks, gluons, tops, bottoms, color, charm, spin and all the other yet to be discovered particles- born of massive collisions at relativistic speeds, swimming in fields of synchrotron radiation.

He would record the merging of new technologies, the marriage of matter and anti-matter, the quest that would lead to the conformation of the Theory of Super-symmetry and the key to creation. Like a scribe in the days of the ancient Pharaohs, he would chronicle events whose shear prominence would carry them forward into the new millennium.

At least that was his intention. If he'd have had any idea of what *really* lay ahead of him, he would have run as far and as fast as his spindly legs could have carried him. Never looking back. Never stopping to catch his breath. Never once turning his head to chance a glimpse of whatever it was that was making those God-awful moaning sounds behind him. And when he could run no more, he'd walk. When he could walk no farther, he'd crawl. If nothing else, he'd just fall forward. Anything that would put one more inch between him and images that would dwell in his mind and haunt his memory forever.

Truly, the light of discovery was burning brightly at Fermilab, but some things are better left in darkness. Some doors should never be opened; they should be bolted shut, FOREVER. That giant accelerator not only unlocked the secrets of matter and energy, it punched a hole through the very fabric of space and time. What emerged from that hole was not of this world, maybe not even of this universe.

The trouble with having a skeleton key is that you can never be sure of what's standing behind the door it unlocks. And as that door creeps open, you may just find that no matter how hard you push, something on the other side pushes back- just a little bit harder. And there's nothing you can do to close it again.

Here then are the events as they unfolded, as Tim Collins recorded them, before the demons were unleashed and the darkness fell.

> **1st Corinthians 1:19** "For it is written. I will destroy the wisdom of the wise, and will bring to nothing the understanding of the prudent."

How To Publish Anything On Amazon's Kindle
By Randy Benjamin

    This is an easy to read, to the point book that explains how to publish your novel, comic book, grocery list, or just about anything else on Amazon's amazing Kindle, and how to do it for practically nothing.

    Let me say that again...this book is "NOT" about how to write your novel, or how to promote it. This isn't a Kindle tips and tricks book and it won't help you to get your book on the New York Times best seller list. This is a, GET ME ON AMAZON so I can SELL MY BOOK...book!

    Other things you need to be aware of are covered in the book as well. Such as...opening a bank account, registering a domain name, setting up a website, designing the cover, writing the description, filing the copyright and adding the copyright page.

    Each step in the Kindle publishing process is explained in a simple and easily understood manner. You won't believe how quickly you can have your book on-line and FOR SALE in the Kindle store.

    How To Publish Anything On Amazon's Kindle is available in paperback and as a Kindle download. For information about the author, visit: www.randybenjamin.com

How To Transfer Cassettes To CD

By Randy Benjamin

The object of this book is to show you how to transfer cassette tapes to CDs with the least amount of hassle.

It's not hard, but it can be confusing considering the various types of cassettes (Type I, II, metal, chrome, etc.) and noise reduction (Dolby and DBX) that might have been in use when the cassette was originally recorded.

In this book, I cover everything you'll need to know to make a quality reproduction. Things such as...selecting the right dubbing cables, input and output jacks, stereo to mono adapters, "Y" adapters and how to make the correct connection.

I'll show you where to find dubbing cables (Radio Shack) and include the catalog numbers and prices. Most transfers can be made using a simple $5 dubbing cable.

It takes special software to transfer your cassettes to the computer but it's available for FREE on the Internet. I'll show you where to find it and how to use it. Actually, everything in this book can be found on the Net for FREE. It's having it gathered in one place and explained in an easily understood manner that gives this book its value.

Cassettes tend to get lost, broken, or just plain wear out. If you've got memories stored on an old cassette, you're at risk of losing them. By transferring them to CD, you'll be able to protect and enjoy them for years to come. For more information on the author, log onto: www.randybenjamin.com.

Original Songs CD
By Randy Benjamin

Long before I became an author, I was a singer/songwriter. I got my first guitar when I was 4 years old. By 7 or 8, I could play it. When I was 13, I wrote my first song. By 18, I was ready to head to Hollywood. That was a magical time in my life. I was a recording artist/songwriter for two major labels, Mercury and Warner Bros. I also recorded for Mike Curb. In fact, Mike signed me to my first recording contract at 19 years of age. He wasn't much older than I was.

Original Songs was released to showcase my original music. The first song on the label, Father's Lullaby, was written for my daughter's wedding. I've recorded another version of it now, Father Daughter Lullaby, and hope to release it around Christmas of 2010. This album has a variety of songs I've written over the years. I've even included a few where I'm playing all of the instruments as well as singing all of the vocal tracks.

I love music. Once music gets in your blood, it's there for good. As much as I love to write, music is still where my roots are deepest.

If you log onto Amazon's search engine and type "Music" under departments and "Randy Benjamin" in the search criteria, you'll find my Original Songs album. Amazon does a great job in marketing. Each song on the album can be sampled by clicking on the 'song' link. In fact, you can even purchase individual songs. I think they're 99 cents each. Audio Samples are on my website as well.

http://www.randybenjamin.com.

Original Songs CD
on Amazon.com

Randy Benjamin
(Netguider)

Sings original songs
for my friends at
SingSnap

Featuring

"Look Into My Eyes"
"Father's Lullaby"

Original Songs

Made in the USA
Middletown, DE
30 March 2018